W9-AFD-839

A Book of One's Own

SECOND EDITION

Second Edition

A Book of One's Own

Developing literacy through making books

Paul Johnson

Graphic illustrator: Jayne Restall

Heinemann
Portsmouth, NH

RETA E. KING LIBRARY

Heinemann
A division of Reed Elsevier Inc.
361 Hanover Street
Portsmouth, NH 03801-3912

Offices and agents throughout the world

First published in 1998 in Great Britain by
Hodder and Stoughton Educational
a division of Hodder Headline Plc
338 Euston Road
London NW1 3BH
GREAT BRITAIN

Also published in the United States of America
in 1998 by Heinemann

**US Cataloging-in-Publication Data is on file with the
Library of Congress**

Johnson, Paul, 1943–
    A book of one's own: developing literacy through making books/
Paul Johnson; graphic illustrator, Jayne Restall.
        p.   cm.
    Includes bibliographical references (p. 126).
    ISBN 0-325-00014-X
    1. Activity programs in education—Great Britain—Handbooks,
manuals, etc.   2. Book design—Study and teaching (Elementary)—
Great Britain—Handbooks, manuals, etc.   3. Child authors—Great
Britain.   I. Title.
LB1027.25.J64   1998
372.133—dc21   98–11236
                                                         CIP

Typeset by Wearset, Boldon, Tyne and Wear
Printed in Great Britain for Hodder & Stoughton Educational, a division
of Hodder Headline Plc, 338 Euston Road, London NW1 3BH by
Redwood Books, Trowbridge, Wiltshire

Contents

Acknowledgements

The author would like to thank the staff and pupils of the following schools for their cooperation in the preparation of this book and allowing him to reproduce books created by them:

Beaver Road Junior School, Manchester.
Birchfields Primary School, Manchester.
Brookburn Primary School, Manchester.
Queens Road Primary School, Stockport.
Broadheath Primary School, Trafford.
Mill Hill Primary School, Oldham.
Hey with Zion Primary School, Oldham.
Sunninghill Primary School, Bolton.
Urmston Infants' School, Trafford.

A special thanks to Beryl Edwards for help in the early years field and Sian Hughes at Gateshouse Books in Manchester.

Introduction

Shortly after *A Book of One's Own* was first published in 1990 the Gulbenkian Foundation funded The Book Art Project (based at The Manchester Metropolitan University) for a two year period. The aim of the project (which was inaugurated by a Crafts Council grant in 1986) is to encourage children to develop their writing through the book form. The publication of this, my first book, together with the Gulbenkian Foundation grant enabled me to present this idea to a wider audience than had previously been possible.

What was particularly attractive to teachers and parents was that most of the book forms suggested in *A Book of One's Own* and subsequently in *Literacy Through the Book Arts* (1993), and *Books Searching for Authors* (1994), could be constructed from single sheets of paper. Many of these books require scissors as the only piece of equipment necessary to make them. Only when sections are cut from *inside* a sheet is a craft knife necessary. Consequently a whole class of children can make them easily and simultaneously.

I could not have imagined in 1990 that over the next few years invitations would come from all over the country and beyond – from Italy, Austria, The Netherlands, Fiji, The Solomon Islands and the USA – for me to run courses for parents and teachers in how to make these books, and how writing could be conceived inside them. Letters come to me daily from around the world which speak of the influence of these books on promoting self-assurance and a sense of achievement in the young when other approaches to communicating on paper have failed. Interest has also come from those working amongst long-stay patients in hospitals (books that can be made in the hand are perfect for someone who is immobile) and a group of East Midlands parents have written to me saying how much these book forms have influenced the strategies they use for teaching their children at home.

As I researched the role of the book arts in education it became evident that making books was not only pleasurable and fulfilling for children, but that it helped them to think and plan what they wanted to say in words and pictures. This element is as relevant to non-fiction as to story writing. In the basic origami book (see page 20) the author is required to organise his or her material into six pages. Whether one is engaged on writing about how to bake a cake, describing the highlights of a holiday, or examining the rain cycle the pupils are conditioned to think in a 'page way' just like professional authors. No other means of writing is quite so successful at this as the book arts!

In revising *A Book of One's Own* I was conscious that its popularity sprung essentially from the book forms it described. For this reason I have replaced some of the original text with new book ideas. Some of them have come from the American paper artist, Edward Hutchins. We started to correspond after becoming aware of each other's work and now a steady exchange of ideas cross the Atlantic. Another consideration when revising this book came from the difficulty some found in interpreting the working diagrams. There is no substitute for being shown in person how to do something; graphic representation is second best. However, I hope that the more complex book forms are easier to follow in this revised edition.

New to this revised edition is the setting of book art in a multicultural context, and consideration of special needs aspects of the genre. I have also provided a section on publishing in the classroom – an area that has gained impetus since I wrote the original book.

People often ask me if I have invented all these books forms. Unfortunately, I am unable to seek a patent on any of them. What a sense of satisfaction I would have felt if I had invented the simple origami book! Eclectically, I have taken ideas from traditional Japanese paper folding and combined them with the innovations of the great nineteenth century German paper engineer, Lothar Meggendorfer. One book found its genesis in a 3-D advertisement in my local building society, and a novel way of folding a table napkin by a restaurant I ate in has been used as the base for more than one book. Everywhere I go I say: please let me have any new book form ideas you come up with. I say the same here. But the book form is meaningless without serious attention given to *what goes inside it*. I cannot stress too forcefully that both technical paper form and written and illustrated content must be seen as one related process. Only then can the book be experienced as a total organism conveying clearly expressed ideas through the magic and wonder of folded paper.

① *Story making for story books*

There have been many arguments for and against the use of the narrative genre in teaching children to write. My own view is that narrative writing embraces so many genres of writing – argument and discussion can feature in stories as well as description and letter writing, and besides, it is part of the child's inheritance and does so much to cultivate imaginative vision. However, it does not follow that the young always find the craft of story writing easy. The imagination does not always behave in a structured way and worst of all, it may fail to function or at least seem paralysed. How many children chew their pencils in class because they can't think what to write? Here are some of the techniques I use to 'release' stories from children and get some kind of structure in the process.

Unlocking the imagination

The rusty door – This most common kind of door is fastened by misuse. But being too insistent on a creative response can be counter-productive: ('Now I want us to think out all the furnishings inside the castle. John, you tell us about the pictures on the walls, and Mary, you tell us what is on the mantelpiece . . .') Children can be frightened by not being able to 'think of something'. Most destructive of all is to tell the class what an unimaginative lot they all are. Children must feel at ease with you, the story conductor. The orchestral conductor does not make the music him or her self but draws music out of the players. A regular story improvisation can do much to facilitate the opening of the imagination's door. The daily 'diary' of the early years classroom in which pupils describe the previous day's events and the next day's expectations is a good preparation for inventing stories. Lazy pupils need prodding and the introverted need coaxing. Of course one must be cautious: quiet or non-communicative children may find it easier to express themselves in writing than talk aloud, and active verbalisers may find difficulty in writing clearly what they have found so easy to say.

The well-oiled door – In nearly every class there is at least one child who is 'good' at telling or creating stories. If you have one of these godsends use him or her as an associate conductor when improvised stories dry up.

Another door is marked **Popular Imagery**. To ask for a character to start a story improvisation can elicit something like Donald Duck or a pop star. Larger than life characters have less story potential than a boy called Alex or a lady called Mrs Thompson. Stereotypes have to be replaced with simple yet convincing images that can be worked on. In an improvisation one might say, 'Well, yes, the president of the USA was there, but who else?'

A door marked **Common Place Imagery** attracts settings like the classroom the pupils are in or a supermarket. There is nothing wrong with these providing they can be seen in a less familiar light, like a noise coming from a classroom cupboard or a supermarket full of magic sauce bottles. Sometimes when accepting a commonplace, say a milkman, I endeavour to winkle out of the class a detailed description of his appearance with asides like – 'Why does he walk with a limp?'

The door marked **Personal Images** reveals characters or situations from stories currently being read by pupils. Is the offered character from the child's imagination or 'lifted' from a book or TV series? Of course story characters can be written about and given new roles to play, but as story conductor one must try to help them have a life of their own.

Somehow every pupil should be involved in making stories however small or insignificant their role. One makes suggestions where necessary, 'stands back' when the story is flowing, injects new ideas when the plot is flagging. The greatest gift a story conductor can bestow is the illusion that the class is making the whole story themselves – that you are an observer not an active creator yourself. Only then will the whole story seem theirs.

Children grow weary easily and have a low threshold of boredom. Timing is therefore crucial to success. So is body language and facial gesture. One can bring alive a character by emphasising the inflections of spoken dialogue, dialect or vocal dynamics: '... and in the field was a box and when Sarah got CLOSE TO IT WHAT SHOULD **SHE FIND BUT** ...'

Making up a story is one thing but turning it into a story book is something else. A description of a book making project with a class of eight year-olds suggests just one way to go about it.

Stories from boxes

From my top pocket I produced a small box-like object. I proceeded to speculate with the class who could have owned it and what it could be used for, before telling them that it was a prayer wheel I had brought back from Darjeeling many years before. We then made up a whole new story about it.

Drafting and presenting

Working in rough books I invited the class to begin again with the box idea but this time to make their own story. As their stories grew they were shared with other pupils, edited and revised and then it was time to transfer them to the concertina book form. It is the simplest book to make and so the most adaptable. In this variation of the form a cover panel is attached to the front of two folded page spreads. Through a window cut in this cover the viewer sees a drawing of the box drawn on the back of the first page. The main episodes into which their stories fell had to be transposed to the folds of the book. We looked at examples of professional writers and illustrators working together and discussed how the story 'fitted' the page.

SELECTING MAIN PARTS OF A STORY

① NAME CHARACTER. HE/SHE GOES SOMEWHERE

② SOMETHING INTERESTING HAPPENS TO HIM/HER

③ WHAT INTERESTING THING HAPPENS NEXT?

HOW DOES THE STORY FINISH?

DO YOU WANT HALF

OR FULL PAGE TEXT?

OR DO YOU WANT TO TRY ANOTHER ARRANGEMENT?

Parts of the story had to be selected for visual presentation. Which events or situations were the most interesting? Should a picture accompany the text? Where on the page should the picture *go*? To help this process page layout suggestions were drawn on the board and pupils selected or invented their own arrangements.

In Andrea's story a lady finds a box on a supermarket shelf. Inside the box is another box and inside that box is a beautiful girl . . .

Continuous concertina book

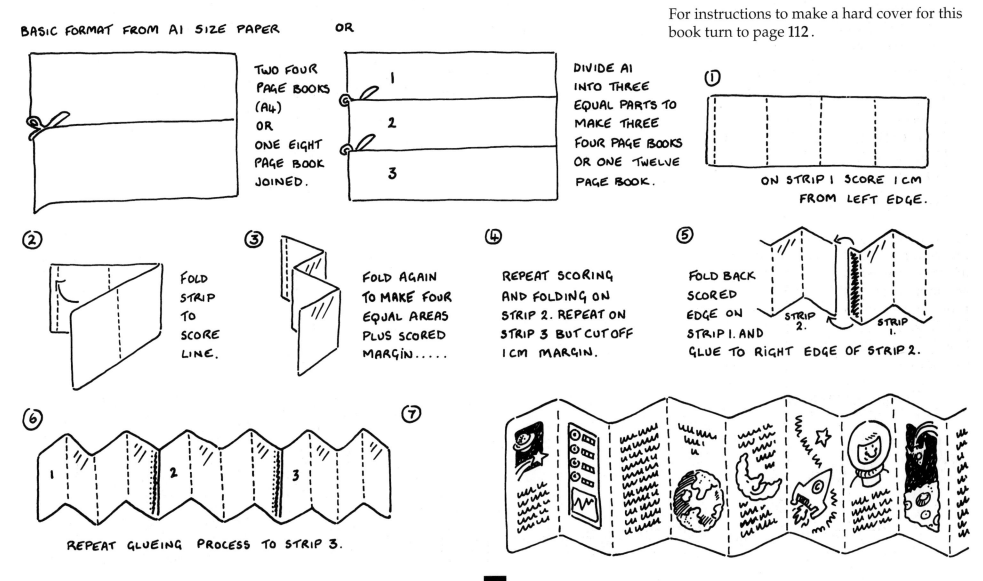

BASIC FORMAT FROM A1 SIZE PAPER   OR

TWO FOUR PAGE BOOKS (A4) OR ONE EIGHT PAGE BOOK JOINED.

1
2
3

DIVIDE A1 INTO THREE EQUAL PARTS TO MAKE THREE FOUR PAGE BOOKS OR ONE TWELVE PAGE BOOK.

For instructions to make a hard cover for this book turn to page 112.

① ON STRIP 1 SCORE 1 CM FROM LEFT EDGE.

② FOLD STRIP TO SCORE LINE.

③ FOLD AGAIN TO MAKE FOUR EQUAL AREAS PLUS SCORED MARGIN.....

④ REPEAT SCORING AND FOLDING ON STRIP 2. REPEAT ON STRIP 3 BUT CUT OFF 1 CM MARGIN.

⑤ FOLD BACK SCORED EDGE ON STRIP 1. AND GLUE TO RIGHT EDGE OF STRIP 2.
STRIP 2.   STRIP 1.

⑥ REPEAT GLUEING PROCESS TO STRIP 3.
1   2   3

⑦

Eight page concertina book

This concertina book is made by following the folding pattern to make eight rectangles described on page 61. When the book is folded down there are a maximum of seven pages to write on and a 'cover' page. The page before last can be the last page of the story or project, or used to give details about the author or a synopsis of the story. The illustration shows the book in its opened-up format.

On the first page of Lee's book he describes all the excitement of being somewhere new. The next page contrasts this with an illustration of him having his breakfast. It is captioned as one might a photograph album. Next is a combined text and illustration page

sketching a day out 'taking pictures', and the last page completes the book with a line drawing of the photograph Lee has taken of the night sky before returning home. The rear side of the concertina holds the cover, and on the far page a drawing of the holiday cottage.

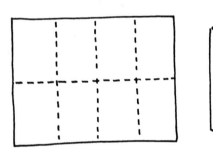

FOLD ON CENTRE HORIZONTALLY AND THEN CONCERTINA INTO FOUR PAGES.

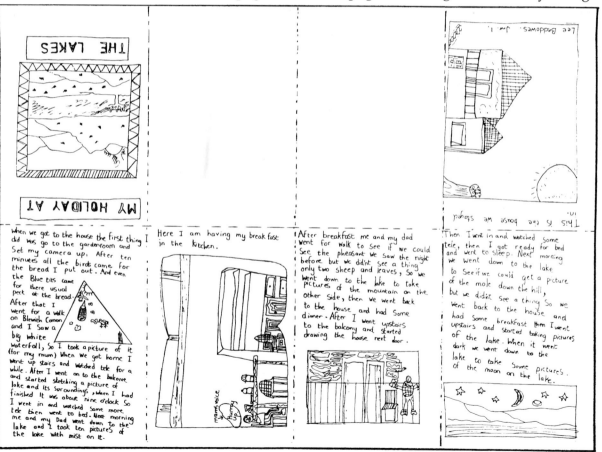

My holiday at the Lakes by Lee (7)

2 Books from one sheet of paper

It is open to debate at what stage a folded birthday-type card can be described as a leaflet, a leaflet a booklet, or a booklet a book. Necessity breeds invention so that which is to be communicated should determine, to some extent at least, the format of the publication. A short poem, depiction or reflection fits neatly into the single fold of the greeting card. An adventure story asks for something more ambitious. Professional graphic designers arrange the copy (words) given to them by a client and accompanying artwork into the constraints of paper size and folded divisions required to fit, for example, things like a standard envelope. Above all, pupils are faced with the challenge of where to place both words and images successfully so they both communicate clearly and look 'good'. The book and book-like forms which follow take the single fold as the point at which a book can take shape. Without a fold we have a poster or single sheet handout. From here endless creative inventions are possible. The golden rule of the Japanese paper folding genre is that nothing is added and nothing taken away from the sheet. I have tried to follow that discipline. It also brings with it other advantages: for example, there is no waste, pages cannot be lost, and cutting multiple book forms (see page 123) is relatively easy. See folding instructions on page 61.

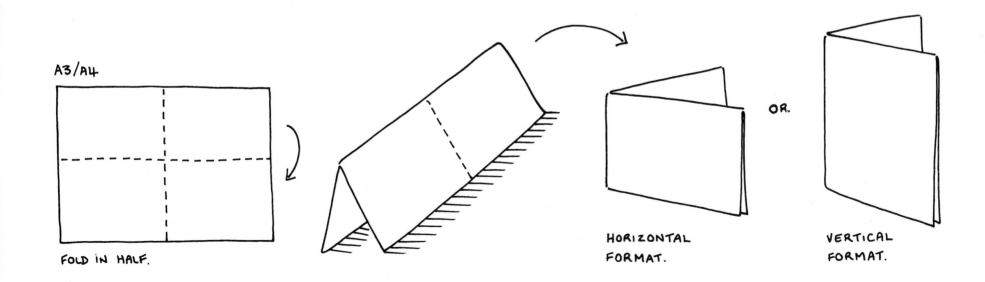

A3/A4

FOLD IN HALF.

HORIZONTAL FORMAT.

OR.

VERTICAL FORMAT.

Folded card with door

An added advantage to the double page is that doors and windows can be cut to provide stimulus for thematic story development. *The Music Soldier* by Daniel (5) shows this to good effect, as does the same strategy in developed form, *The Castle House* by Jennifer (6).

'The Music Soldier' by Daniel (5)

the soldier is playing music he is in the tings band with a trumpet

'The Castle House' by Jennifer (6) Door closed . . . Door open . . .

THE Castle House

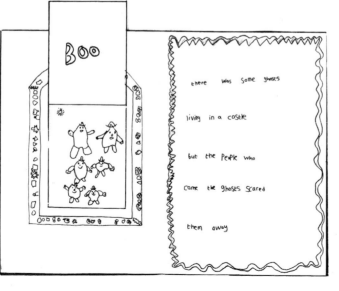

Boo

there was some ghosts

living in a castle

but the peapl who

came the ghosts scared

them away

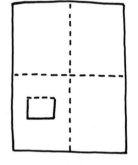

OPEN FLAP TO REVEAL ARTWORK BENEATH.

'The Monster' by John (8)

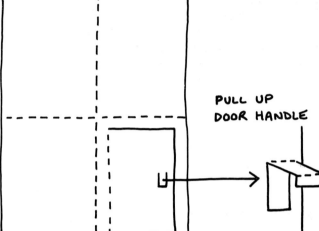

PULL UP
DOOR HANDLE

The Monster by John (8) intensifies the door theme by cutting a pull-up door handle. The quality of John's artwork has been stimulated by the novelty of the folded presentation.

This design stimulates a single folded story which is hidden and therefore thematically secret, private or in Andrew's case, ghostly. To augment the mood of ghostliness everything is back to front; the booklet opens from right to left and all the writing inside is from right to left too!

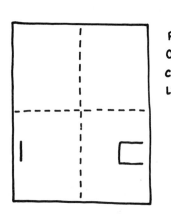

① FOLD A3 AS SHOWN. ON BOTTOM RIGHT PANEL CUT DOOR WITH CORRESPONDING LEFT PANEL SLOT.

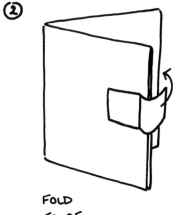

② FOLD TO A5. FOLD DOOR FLAP AROUND ....

③ AND LOCK INTO SLOT ON REVERSE.

'Ghost Hunter Secret File' by Andrew (8)

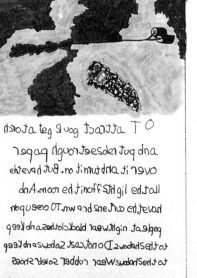

4 *Window card*

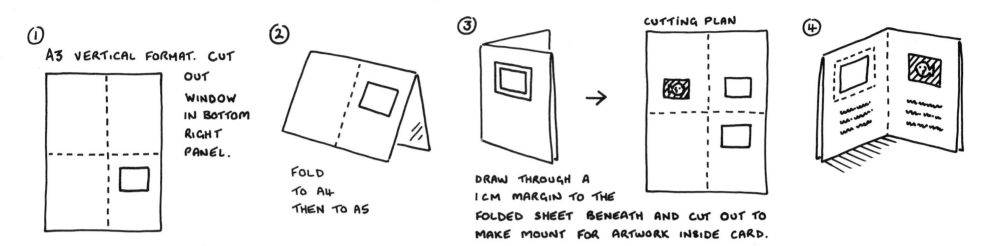

① A3 VERTICAL FORMAT. CUT OUT WINDOW IN BOTTOM RIGHT PANEL.

② FOLD TO A4 THEN TO A5

③ DRAW THROUGH A 1CM MARGIN TO THE FOLDED SHEET BENEATH AND CUT OUT TO MAKE MOUNT FOR ARTWORK INSIDE CARD.

CUTTING PLAN

④

This method of presentation produces a double mounted piece of artwork supported by writing. Moira (9) made a white line on coloured background illustration of a small trinket box in the shape of a duck. This was made by inscribing the design with a hard pencil (HB,1H) through tracing paper to cartridge beneath. This makes a light incision in the cartridge which can be crayoned over to produce the unique white line effect shown. The finished artwork was glued into the picture area, the story written to accompany it and a title incorporated into the cover design. Finally, a decorative border was applied to the mounted area.

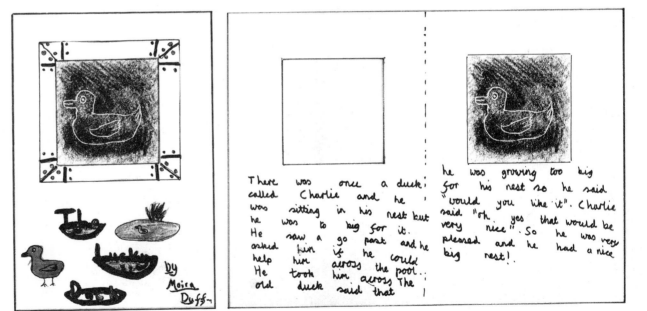

Cover

Inside card

⑤ Presentation card

This is an attractive locked card suitable for invitations and celebrations.

①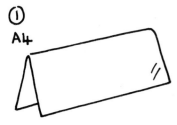

A4

FOLD ON HORIZONTAL.

②

MAKE LOOP OF STRIP, ENSURING THAT FOLDS ARE AVOIDED.

③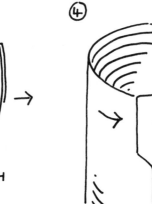

CUT "V" SLOT THROUGH THE FOUR SHEETS.

④

OPEN STRIP AND LOCK INTO CYLINDER

⑤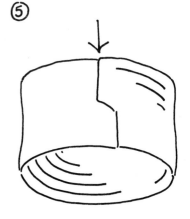

WITH LOCK IN THE CENTRE PRESS CYLINDER FLAT TO FORM CARD.

⑥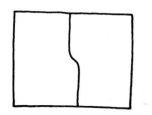

VARIATIONS :-

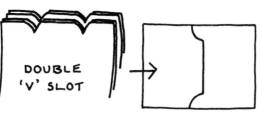

DOUBLE 'V' SLOT

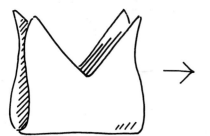 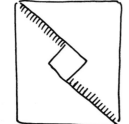

EXTRA LARGE "V" SLOT

Invitation card designed by Stuart (8).

Haiku poem fold and origami envelope

Before moving on to the next stage of basic books, I want to include a very intimate interrelationship of two sheets of A4 paper. The simplicity of beauty is so inspiringly manifested in the Haiku poem (lines of 5,7,5 syllables) and what could be more appropriate than a simple origami envelope to hold the words?

John (9) wrote:

'When the day is gone
The moon and stars shine brightly
And dreams fill the world.'

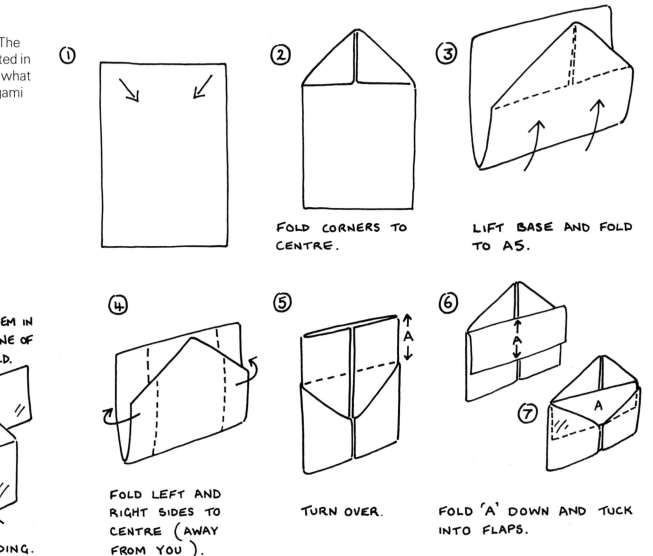

①

② FOLD CORNERS TO CENTRE.

③ LIFT BASE AND FOLD TO A5.

④ FOLD LEFT AND RIGHT SIDES TO CENTRE (AWAY FROM YOU).

⑤ TURN OVER.

⑥ ⑦ FOLD 'A' DOWN AND TUCK INTO FLAPS.

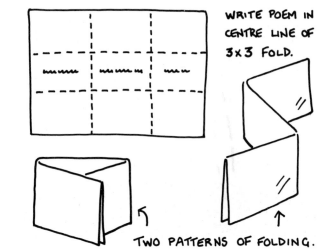

WRITE POEM IN CENTRE LINE OF 3×3 FOLD.

TWO PATTERNS OF FOLDING.

Tabernacle card

Here two 'doors' of equal proportion enclose a
back panel with vaulted roof.

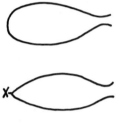

① A4 HORIZONTAL

FOLD OUTER EDGES TO
CENTRE. TO FIND CENTRE
WITHOUT CREASING
PAPER MAKE A LOOP.
MARK HALFWAY POINT
ALONG TOP EDGE WITH
FINGERNAIL 'X'.

②

③ FOLD CORNERS TO CENTRE

④ FOLD CORNERS BACK AND PUSH INWARDS

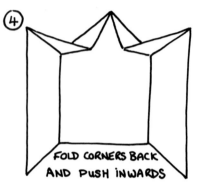

When laid top-down, Kate (8) thought that the
form looked like a frog. This stimulated frog
artwork on the outside central panel, and a story
'The Ferocious Frog' on the outside (door) panels.

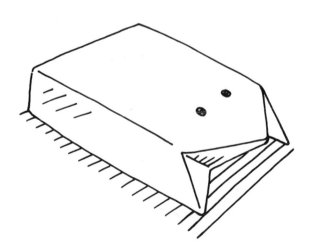

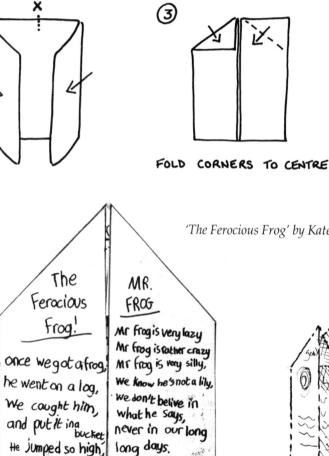

'The Ferocious Frog' by Kate (8)

The Ferocious Frog!

Once we got a frog,
he went on a log,
We caught him,
and put it in a bucket.
He jumped so high,
and looked at the sky,
and splashed.
I said "into the pond
chuck it."
HE JUMPED OUT.

MR. FROG

Mr Frog is very lazy
Mr frog is rather crazy
Mr Frog is very silly,
We know he's not a lily,
we don't belive in
what he says,
never in our long
long days.

Sarah (8) invented this one – 'The Magic Tree Seed' – a series of concertina folds which increase in size. Her story, about a growing tree, prompted the book's invention, so that 'the book could grow like a tree'.

'The Magic Tree Seed' by Sarah (8)

FOLD ON HORIZONTAL.

A4

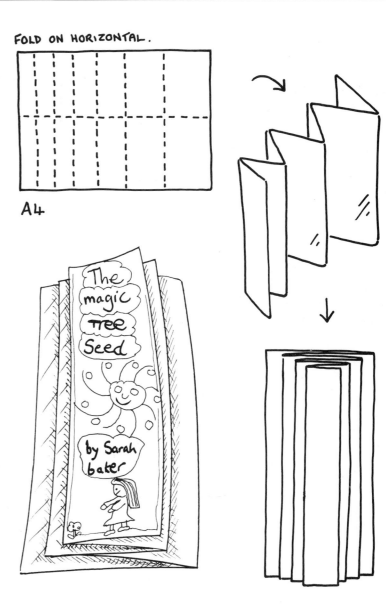

Origami book

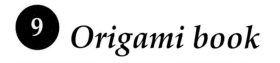

The simplicity of this book makes it immediately accessible for large-class production whilst being more novel than a simple folded concertina. If children are capable of using scissors, they can make the whole book themselves. I must have seen several hundred origami books by children, on every conceivable theme from stories to recipes, local studies to illustrated journals.

'My Best Friend' by Lisa (6)

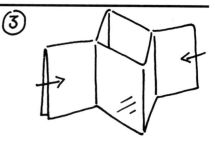

① CREASE TO EIGHT PANELS. OPEN SHEET. FOLD IN HALF AND CUT ON FOLDED EDGE TO HALF WAY POINT.

② OPEN SHEET AND FOLD ON LANDSCAPE HORIZONTAL.

③ PUSH LEFT AND RIGHT ENDS TO CENTRE.

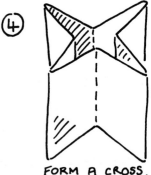

④ FORM A CROSS.

⑤ FOLD ROUND TO FORM BOOK. SIX WRITING/ ARTWORK PAGES, FRONT AND BACK COVERS.

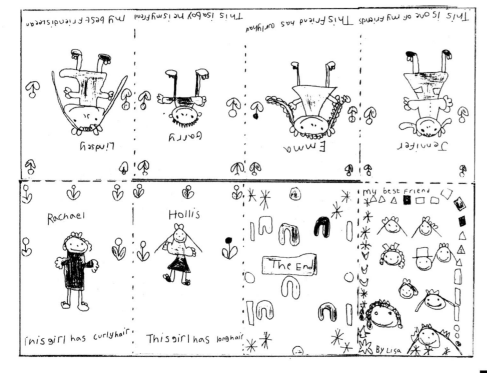

One of the fascinating things about the origami book is that it can be presented as a three-dimensional form. Leo's *Flying House*, a variation of the origami house book, is displayed like an architect's model. If wished, the inside of the building can be drawn too. The building can be conceived as 'My House' or 'The Magic House' with the narrative written on the side panels. In a geographical context the theme could be 'Houses in Other Parts of the World' and in a religious studies context mosques, synagogues and churches can be made in a similar way.

Flying house by Leo (6)

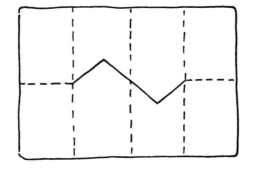

CREASE SHEET VERTICALLY IN HALF AND HALF AGAIN IN THE SAME DIRECTION. OPEN SHEET. DRAW A LINE THROUGH THE CENTRE AND CUT PANELS AS SHOWN.

FOLLOW DIAGRAMS 2 AND 3 FROM 'ORIGAMI' BOOK.

Other variations of the three-dimensional origami book include this castle which could make a history project more realistic. By cutting side panels and doors the basic castle can be made more complex.

①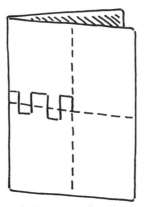

FOLLOW SAME CREASING
INSTRUCTIONS AS ORIGAMI
HOUSE BOOK AND CUT AS SHOWN.

②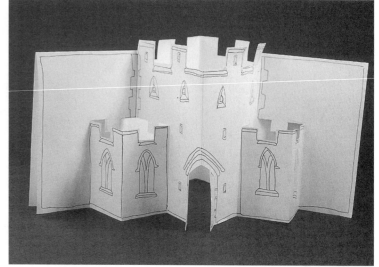

FOLLOW DIAGRAMS
2 AND 3 FROM 'ORIGAMI BOOK'.

DEVELOPMENTAL DESIGN . . . .

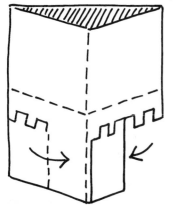

OPEN SHEET AND FOLD LEFT AND RIGHT
EDGES TO CENTRE. IN BOTTOM PANELS
CUT AS SHOWN. CREASE SECTIONS TO CENTRE.

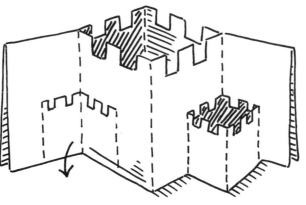

OPEN SHEET AND FOLD AS BEFORE.
PULL OUT SIDE BUILDINGS.

Story and pictures in 3 triangular sequences . . .

One of the conventions of basic, one-sheet books is that the pages tend to be of the A5 format. A way of arriving at a different shape book from an A2 base is as follows:

① FOLD CORNER TO EDGE AND REPEAT FROM TOP CORNER TO FORM DIAGONAL CROSS.

② MAKE VERTICAL CREASES AT 'A' AND HORIZONTAL CREASE AT 'B'. CUT AS SHOWN.

③ FOLD TRIANGLE 'X' 'UNDER OVER' UNTIL FORM IS COMPLETED.

④ FOLD LEFT PANEL FORWARD.

⑤ COMPLETED BOOK.

Open first page

Front cover ⑥

'The Flower Lady' by Jennie (9)

⑦

This is another book which was stimulated by experimental illustrations. The technique is to cut forms – tree, house, figure – from fairly thick cartridge and then make a 'frottage' rubbing with wax crayons through thinner paper placed on top. The surface quality this gives is quite different to any other technique and lends itself well to book illustration (see page 35). Jennie's cut-outs for 'The Flower Lady' were a flower, sweet, and a cat, and these illustrations evoke a fantasy world which inspired an imaginative, dreamy environment in which her story could take shape.

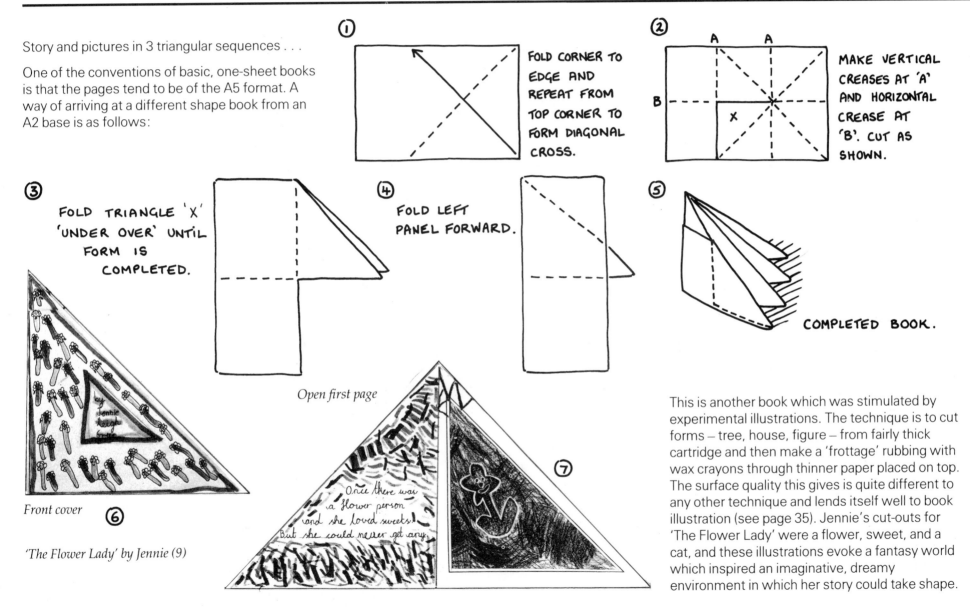

One of the most popular single sheet books with children is described next. A conventional four-fold concertina book is made from horizontally folded A2, but instead of leaving the pages blank, hinged openings are cut into the four folds. This approach has already been discussed, but here I show a more developed way of working.

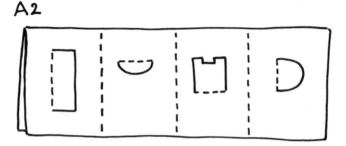

A2

HINGED OPENINGS GIVEN
TO THE CLASS AS A SOURCE
OF STORY STIMULATION.

'Blast Off' by Matthew and Davydd (10) (openings closed)

FOOD SUPLY   Engine window

Shut the air-lock door.
Get ready for blast-off.
5,4,3,2,1.
Blast off

Here is moon beam
Freadie, the astronaut
See what he looks like.
Smile back!

Landing on the moon,
we see a castle.
Argh, we see an alien
Let's run!

Phew! we escaped

In the space ship.
Ready for blast-off
5,4,3,2,1.
We are now in space.
Look at Earth.

Experiment by cutting folded doors, windows and openings into the bottom panels as shown. An added challenge is to cut shapes in a free, unpreconceived way. The task is then to give meaning to them in story form. This form of presentation is exemplified by two groups using the same shaped openings. What is fascinating is the contrasting imagery derived from them (see next page). The dedication to design, layout, handwriting and story illustrates just how powerful an incentive an imaginatively prepared challenge is to children.

Cover design

Openings open

'The Teddy Bears Picnic'
by Karen and Lisa (10)

Doors closed

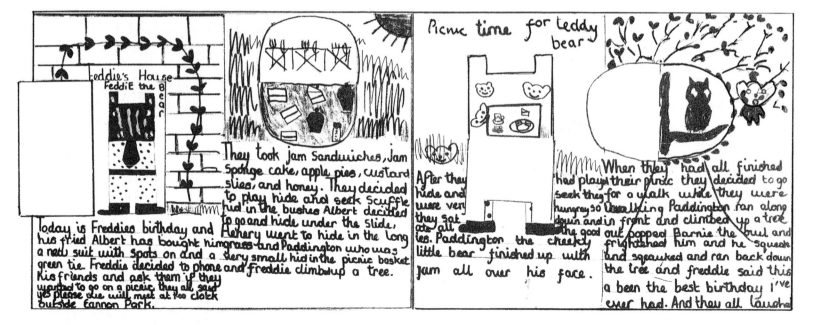

Doors open

Another 3D book, but of a much simpler kind, returns to the diminishing door theme.

When the concertina doors are stood on end vertically and pulled down over page 4 of the bottom concertina, a vista is created through the arcade of openings.

Andrew (8) has exploited this 'peep show' effect to good use in his book 'Treasure in the House of Horrors'. Here, the diminishing doors revealed what appeared to be a sports car, but on closer inspection turned out to be a cannon.

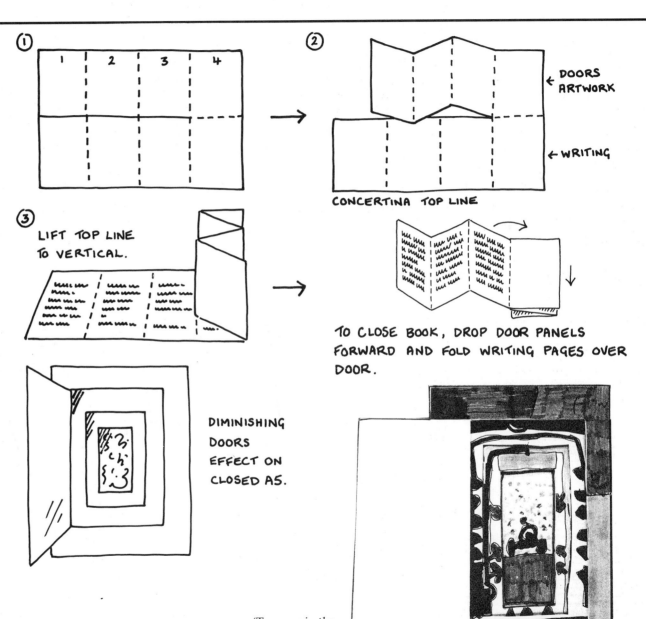

① 1 2 3 4

② ← DOORS ARTWORK

← WRITING

CONCERTINA TOP LINE

③ LIFT TOP LINE TO VERTICAL.

TO CLOSE BOOK, DROP DOOR PANELS FORWARD AND FOLD WRITING PAGES OVER DOOR.

DIMINISHING DOORS EFFECT ON CLOSED AS.

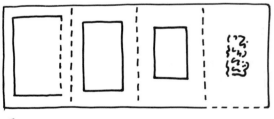

TOP LINE ARTWORK (BACK VIEW)

TOP LINE ARTWORK (FRONT VIEW)

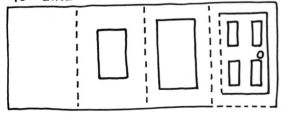

'Treasure in the House of Horrors' (folded down) by Andrew (8)

The opening 'door and window'-style book can be engineered as a single page presentation. I am indebted to Janet, one of my BEd students, for this invention.

Although the prospect of cutting so many apertures is a daunting proposition, using the multiple cutting technique quickens the process of manufacture for a whole class. A simpler approach would be to reduce the number of openings.

This is possibly the most complex of the books suggested here, although the cutting and folding procedure is really quite simple. In Matthew's book, he traces a journey into Dracula's wardrobe to the glass where he keeps his false teeth!

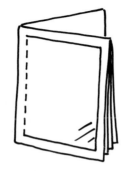

FOLD A2 TO A5s

DRAW DOOR ON FRONT OF BOOK, OPEN OUT AND CUT.
FOLD DOWN AGAIN TO A5. OPEN DOOR AND DRAW
THROUGH NO 2 DOOR.
REPEAT PROCESS TO DOOR NO 7.

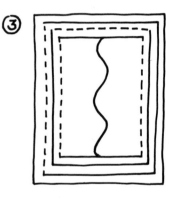

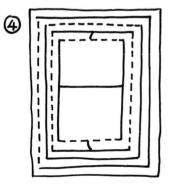

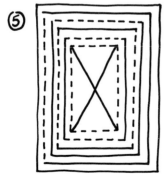

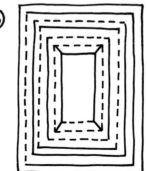

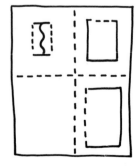

SIMPLIFIED A3 VERSION
USING 3 DOORS.

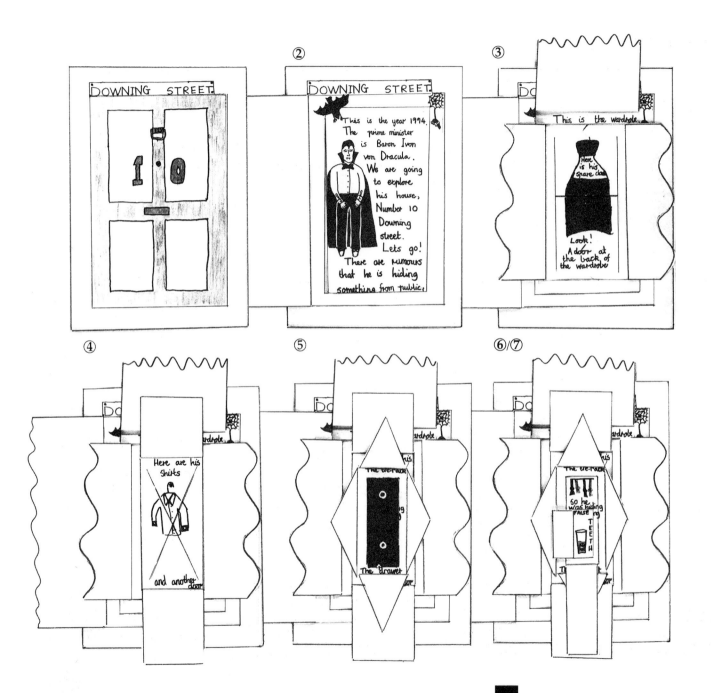

'Downning Street' by Matthew (10)

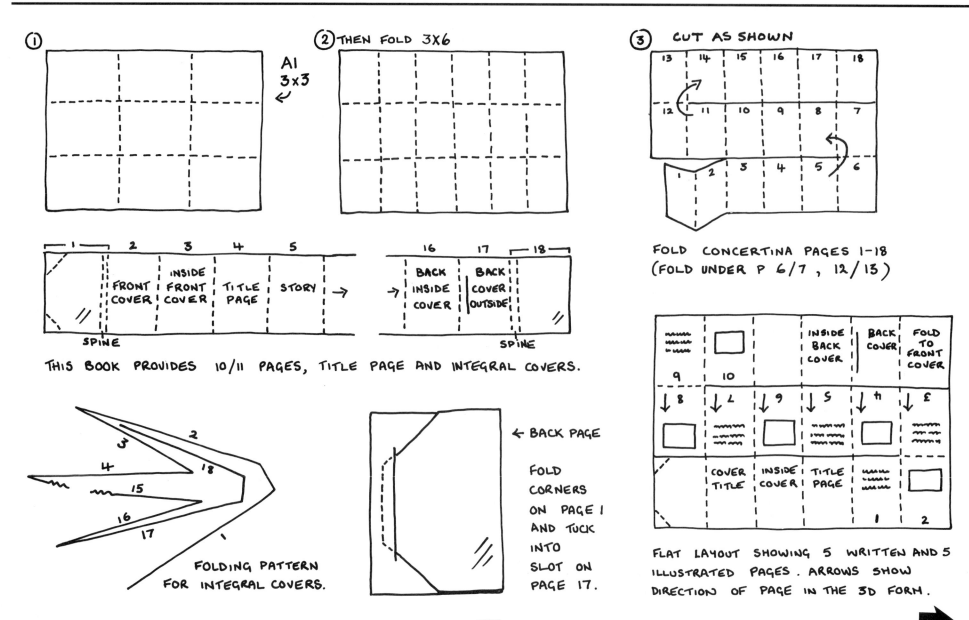

①

A1
3x3 ←

② THEN FOLD 3X6

③ CUT AS SHOWN

13	14	15	16	17	18
12	11	10	9	8	7
1	2	3	4	5	6

1	2	3	4	5
	FRONT COVER	INSIDE FRONT COVER	TITLE PAGE	STORY →

SPINE

16	17	18
→ BACK INSIDE COVER	BACK COVER OUTSIDE	

SPINE

THIS BOOK PROVIDES 10/11 PAGES, TITLE PAGE AND INTEGRAL COVERS.

FOLD CONCERTINA PAGES 1-18
(FOLD UNDER P 6/7, 12/13)

FOLDING PATTERN FOR INTEGRAL COVERS.

← BACK PAGE

FOLD CORNERS ON PAGE 1 AND TUCK INTO SLOT ON PAGE 17.

FLAT LAYOUT SHOWING 5 WRITTEN AND 5 ILLUSTRATED PAGES. ARROWS SHOW DIRECTION OF PAGE IN THE 3D FORM.

This arrangement of three A5 pages to front and back strengthens the cover. The beauty of this book is that the whole book, including covers, is produced as part of the integral folding of the A1 sheet.

'The Change of the Old Lady' – Clare (10) thought of a character and then placed five sheets of rough paper in front of her to represent the stages of the book's development:

Page 1 – An old lady called Mrs Bennett buys sweets in a sweetshop but then her top half turns into a giant pencil.

Page 2 – The shopkeeper runs out of the shop frightened, but then the bottom half of Mrs Bennett turns into a window.

Page 3 – The shopkeeper returns and is about to give Mrs Bennett her sweets when the whole of her turns into a blackboard.

Page 4 – The shopkeeper is angry with all these transformations, but Mrs Bennett suggests that it is he who is seeing things and not her changing.

Page 5 – Eventually Mrs Bennett resumes her natural self and gets her sweets.

This evidences a strategy for compiling a story to fit a ready-made book. It was prepared in stages: (*i*) selecting subject and thematic environment; (*ii*) spacing out development to set number of changes related to (*iii*) story 'shape':

Statement (page 1)
Development (pages 2,3)
'Twist' (page 4)
Resolution (page 5)

BOOK 'EXPLODED'

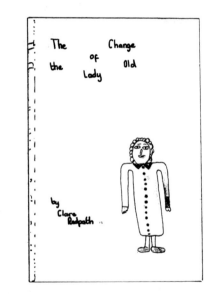

'The change of the old lady' by Clare (10)

The completed drafting exercise led to the 'writing in' of the story, followed by illustrations. Finally, title page and cover design completed the book.

This method is similar to the previous book (on page 48) except fewer pages are folded from the base sheet. I gave this book to Louise (11) and asked her to make a story to fit it. Originally it was decided that the cover would be included, integrally, but later a separate cover was added. This accounts for the book having two title pages!

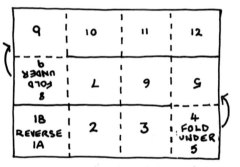

FOLD AS BEFORE. DESIGNATE PAGES AS DIAGRAM. NOTE FOLD1 IS USED ON BOTH SIDES HENCE 1A/B

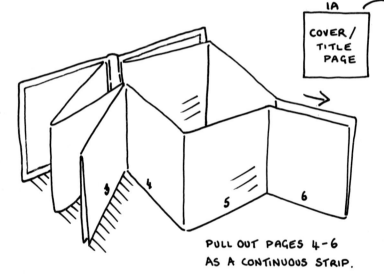

PULL OUT PAGES 4–6 AS A CONTINUOUS STRIP.

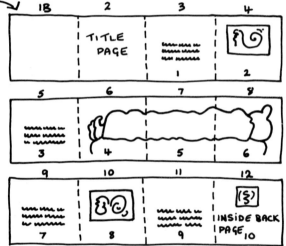

FOLD NUMBERS AT TOP OF PAGES.

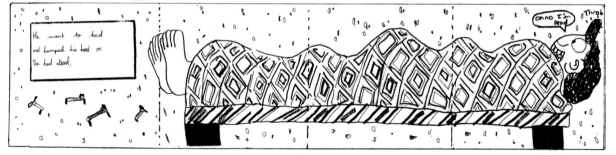

'The Man from Peru' by Louise (11) (artwork on pull out pages 4–6)

Louise discovered that, because of the way the book is folded, page 4–5 can be pulled out as a continuous strip. So already the book's design was making demands on the author. Pages 4, 5 and 6 were therefore designated as a pull-out illustration and the remaining pages were allocated roles as shown – four story and six illustration pages. From the first encounter, it was clear that Louise was going to approach the book in a humorous vein. 'What a crazy book!' she said, and who could disagree with her?

'The Man from Peru' uses rhyme to propel the imagery along.

(1) There was a man from Peru/Who lived on a lou (sic). (3) He went to bed and bumped his head on the bedstead. (7) He dreamed about getting wed. (9) And woke up thinking he was dead.

All this was composed alongside the empty book format, so that corresponding rough draft pages were prepared for writing and graphic work. The idea of pages 4–6 containing a bed prompted the head/bedstead rhyme. The style of graphic, comic strip imagery has come from popular publishing, but the iconic forms are never stereotypical: they manage to be alive and personal. We discussed design and layout – assymetric balance of words and images and ways of organising the book's design. So the book came into being in stage by stage transfers from final draft to book presentation. The completed book was given a thin white card wrap around cover.

Wrap around cover design

Beginning of story

We discussed design and layout

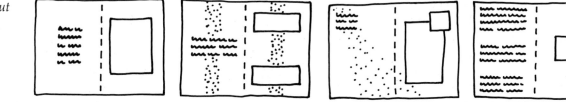

A2 3×4

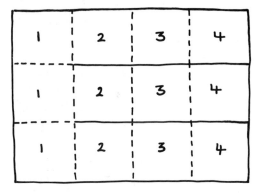

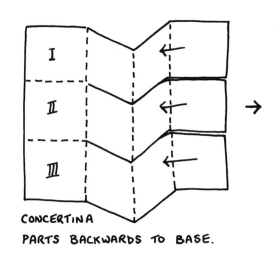

CONCERTINA
PARTS BACKWARDS TO BASE.

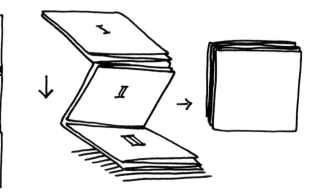

CONCERTINA THREE SECTIONS
DOWNWARDS.

Cut-out book illustration (student)

Another cutting pattern on the same 3 × 4 fold produces a book in three pull-out sections.

It is so easy for children's illustrative and design work to be limited to pen and pencil work. Always employing examples of excellence from the commercial presses in my teaching, I used for this project Jan Pienkowski's beautifully designed *Easter* (Heinemann, 1989) with black cut-out illustrations.

Nick (10) liked doing cartoon-type drawings, but for his book I persuaded him to have a go at silhouette figures in black paper. The more he investigated the technique, the deeper his involvement in the mysterious visual power of the solid black image on white, as his work will testify. This is another example of the intuitive sense of design that children have. How well the shapes and 'psychological relationships' of the figures and objects exist in the spatial field of the page. So Nick found in front of him a three part book waiting to be transformed into a story. The synopsis of his story is as follows: Nick is sent out shopping and sees what he believes to be a dead body but it turns out to be a coat. In his excitement he forgets what he is sent out for and returns home empty handed.

As he prepared the story for the book he found that it fitted more naturally into three sequences of three. His solution to this was to fill the last panel of each part with a white on black motif.

REAR PAGE 4 (BOTTOM PART)
GLUED TO INSIDE BACK COVER.

PART NUMBERS
WRITTEN
ON THE BACK
OF WHITE
ON BLACK
SILHOUETTES.

'Going to the shops' by Nick (10)

A development of the basic origami and multi-fold concertina book is the Tall Story Book. This comprises horizontally-folded A3 divided into six parts.

The format gives an elongated page shape, hence the title. The special feature of the design is that page 5 tucks back to allow the open top fold (6) to fold around it. This produces an open-up section of three pages: 6,7,8. In the prescribed book, a simple recognisable shape is drawn on page 6 which is then continued on the other two adjacent flaps (7,8) by the author. The challenge here is for the author to invent the continuation from page 6 – to the beginning, and the end!

Robin's 'Raiders of the Best Museum' was preoccupied with Tutankhamen when this 'Tall Book' project began and so he adapted the format to accommodate the topic of the ancient Egyptians. Again the style of writing and graphic presentation has been influenced by strip cartoons. The prepared image on page 6 is conceived as a rock, although the reader is led to believe it is a bone. By setting the story around the disappearance of Tutankhamen's left elbow bone from a museum invites reader participation: 'Can you guess what the picture on page 6 is? Turn the page and find out.'

Pages 9–11 conclude the story by the protagonist 'Super Pharoah' returning the bone to the museum.

A3

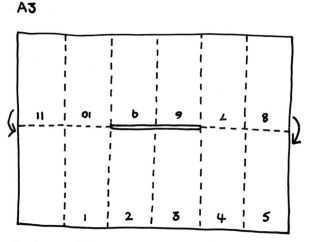

FOLD DOWN.

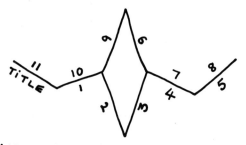

PLAN.

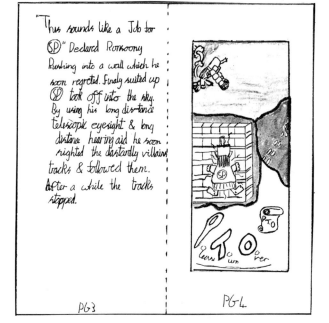

Page from 'Raiders of the Best Museum' by Robin (9)

The challenge for the reader is to guess what the continued form is before opening the flaps 7 and 8. This feature is the pivotal point of the book for the image conceived diverts the story forward to page 1 and to page 11.

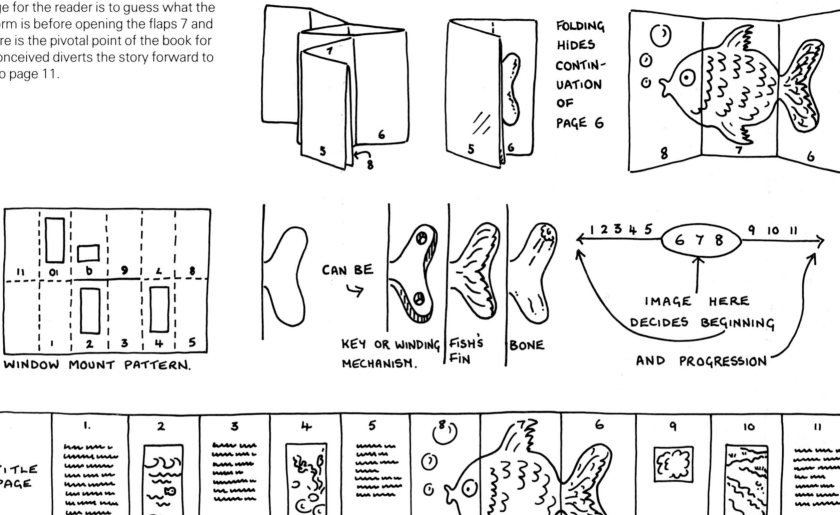

FOLDING HIDES CONTINUATION OF PAGE 6

PLAN

WINDOW MOUNT PATTERN.

CAN BE

KEY OR WINDING MECHANISM.

FISH'S FIN

BONE

1 2 3 4 5   6 7 8   9 10 11

IMAGE HERE DECIDES BEGINNING

AND PROGRESSION

TITLE PAGE

1. 2 3 4 5 8 7 6 9 10 11

Because of the design of the central image, pages 6, 7 and 8 run in reverse to the chronological order. Pages for writing are faced with illustration pages with additional pages for either writing or images.

Binding – The title is hinged to the inside front of a wrap around cover. All the other pages need to be left free so there is no back page attachment.

Illustrations from Robin's book showing the opening out 6–8 sequence

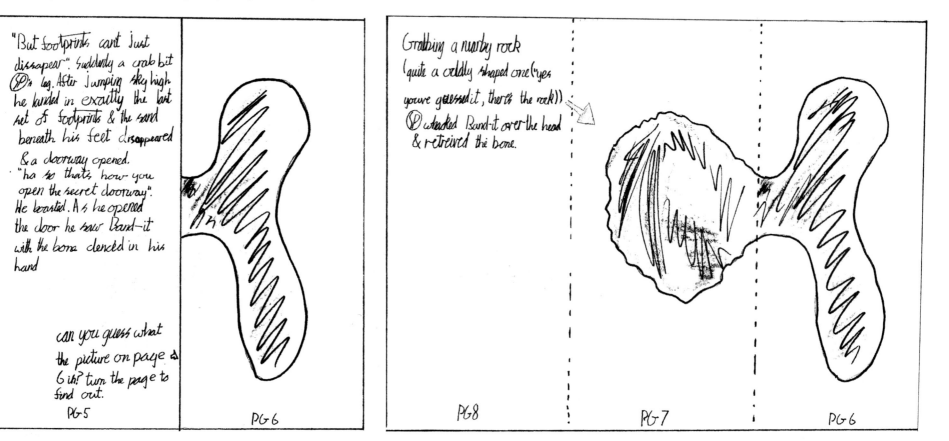

This book is the result of another experiment with paper cutting and folding. A door has been cut into one of the folds and then the sheet is concertina-folded as shown.

Adele turned the pages of her ready-made book and decided on the front as title page, pages 1, 2 and 3 as story, but then she puzzled over the remaining three pages because they were all joined together. We discussed possible ways of using this in her story but, as so often happens, the 'door' symbol took charge of her thinking and these pages portrayed a series of doors leading, in effect, out of the book. Working backwards from these doors into the story, she was required to devise a plot on three, approximately 15 cm square pages. Her idea of John tyring to escape from the book is carefully constructed to fit the dimensions of the pages.

The finished book was bound into a simple wrap around cover and a fourth door cut into the back, enabling John to finally escape.

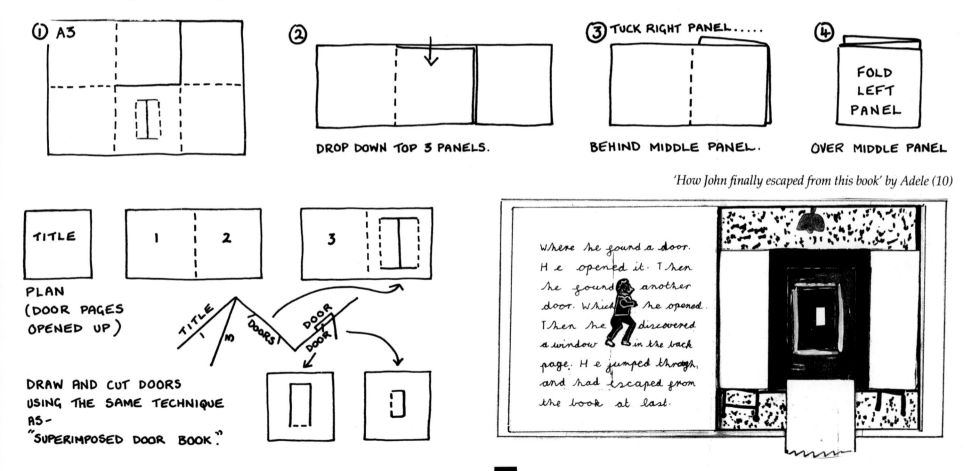

'How John finally escaped from this book' by Adele (10)

Where he found a door. He opened it. Then he found another door. Which he opened. Then he discovered a window in the back page. He jumped through, and had escaped from the book at last.

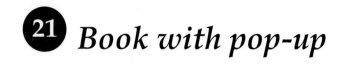

This is one of the first experimental books I made from a single sheet of paper, and it has remained one of the most popular with children.

Stage 1

① **A2**

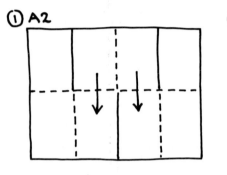

②

B			A
B	B	A	A

DROP TOP MIDDLE FLAP FORWARDS.

③

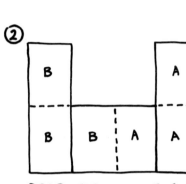

FOLD 'A' OVER 'B'. FOLD OUTER FLAPS TOWARDS CENTRE.

④

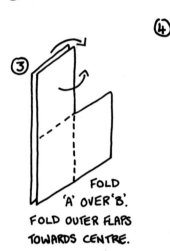

DROP TOP SINGLE FLAPS DOWN. TURN TO HORIZONTAL POSITION.

⑤ OPEN BOOK COVER

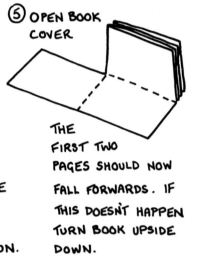

THE FIRST TWO PAGES SHOULD NOW FALL FORWARDS. IF THIS DOESN'T HAPPEN TURN BOOK UPSIDE DOWN.

Stage 2

ORDERING PAGE SEQUENCE

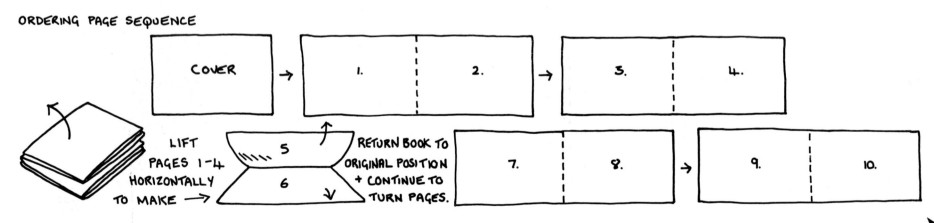

| COVER | → | 1. | 2. | → | 3. | 4. |

LIFT PAGES 1-4 HORIZONTALLY TO MAKE →

5 / 6

RETURN BOOK TO ORIGINAL POSITION + CONTINUE TO TURN PAGES.

| 7. | 8. | → | 9. | 10. |

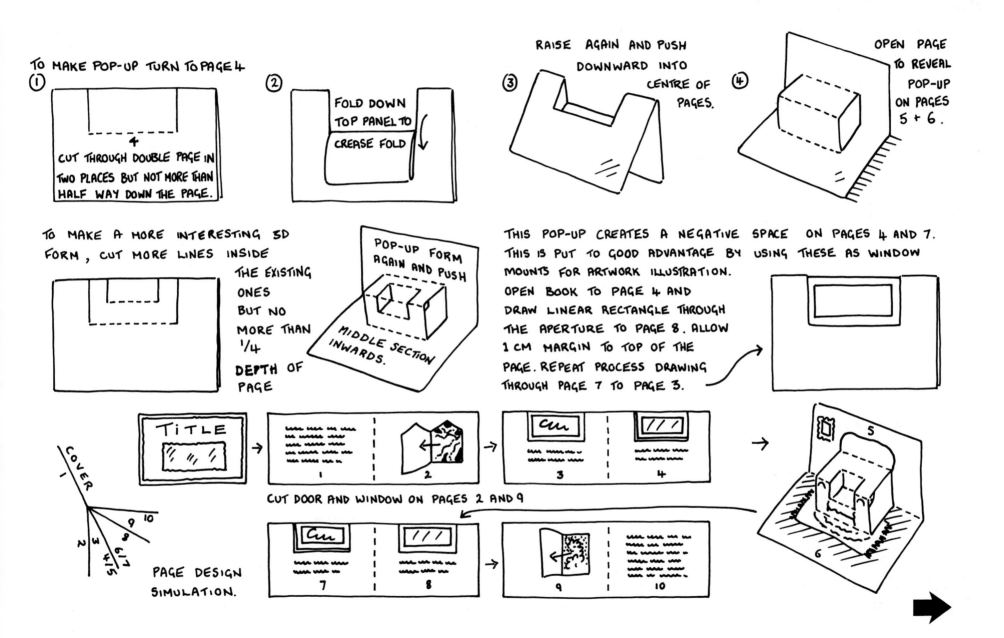

TO MAKE POP-UP TURN TO PAGE 4
① CUT THROUGH DOUBLE PAGE IN TWO PLACES BUT NOT MORE THAN HALF WAY DOWN THE PAGE.

4

② FOLD DOWN TOP PANEL TO CREASE FOLD

③ RAISE AGAIN AND PUSH DOWNWARD INTO CENTRE OF PAGES.

④ OPEN PAGE TO REVEAL POP-UP ON PAGES 5 + 6.

TO MAKE A MORE INTERESTING 3D FORM, CUT MORE LINES INSIDE THE EXISTING ONES BUT NO MORE THAN 1/4 DEPTH OF PAGE

POP-UP FORM AGAIN AND PUSH MIDDLE SECTION INWARDS.

THIS POP-UP CREATES A NEGATIVE SPACE ON PAGES 4 AND 7. THIS IS PUT TO GOOD ADVANTAGE BY USING THESE AS WINDOW MOUNTS FOR ARTWORK ILLUSTRATION. OPEN BOOK TO PAGE 4 AND DRAW LINEAR RECTANGLE THROUGH THE APERTURE TO PAGE 8. ALLOW 1 CM MARGIN TO TOP OF THE PAGE. REPEAT PROCESS DRAWING THROUGH PAGE 7 TO PAGE 3.

COVER

PAGE DESIGN SIMULATION.

TITLE

CUT DOOR AND WINDOW ON PAGES 2 AND 9

The book is almost mirror-imaged, the pop-up middle section being the pivot. The number of writing lines to each page depends upon the stage of development of the children. For a class of six- or seven-year-olds one or two lines might represent an acceptable number of words, whereas a whole page of writing might be expected of top juniors. (Of course, quantity does not equate with quality, but I use these as a rough guide when designing writing pages.)

I first explored this book form with a class of year five pupils. Each had a blank book in front of them and we went through my simulation page by page. We discussed what could happen through doors and windows and how these ideas could influence the crafted story. The central pop-up was inevitably the climax and we brainstormed a multitude of things: a cubic form could be a chair, throne, box, car, or house. An unfortunate condition of the pop-up form put to

good use is the negative space it makes. The open area has been utilised as a window for illustrations on pages 3 and 8. This produces the same illustration on page 8 as page 4, and page 7 as page 3. This requires two pieces of artwork to be accommodated by four pieces of writing.

It is a very challenging book form but one to which the children responded at once with excitement. They numbered the pages of their jotters 1–10, corresponding to the book's pages and then set about the rough draft of the story. They were at liberty to illustrate (from rough sketches) at any point during the project.

Some found that the story idea could be conceptualised more clearly by being drawn first, whilst others preferred to complete the writing first. But the general pattern of creative behaviour was for the story drafting/writing and illustration to be processed concurrently. Perhaps the biggest challenge was to provide two illustrations to fit the four pages of writing.

Rough draft jotters correspond to the blank book pages

Panda Bear

One day Panda - Bear was eating his bamboo, Hoot Hoot was near by eating a worm "Munch Munch" As they were eating they heard parrot calling "hey Hoot Hoot parrot is calling" cried Panda Bear, so they ran off to meet him. "Hey parrot" what is it" asked Panda-Bear. Parrot told them that there was a strange door at the west side of the jungle.

1

Panda-Bear packed a few bamboo canes and off they went. Half way there they stoped for lunch. When they got up it was nearly Noon so they hurried off and they arrived 3 hours later, There in froint of them was a big Red and blue door "shall we go through" said parrot "why not" said panda-Bear!

2

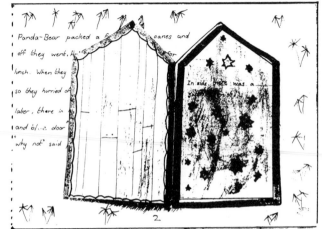

Panda-Bear packed a f... canes and off they went. H... ...for lunch. When they ... so they hurried of... later, there in ... and b/... door "why not" said

2

Door open

They couldn't believe their. eyes they were in the desert. The desert was 9 degrees and only one palm tree in sight. There was sand on sand, Sand every re" hey" cried panda Bear "it's to hot" lets get out of here. So they ran and ran and ran and soon they came to this window!

A window in the middle of the sky through the window they could see the North pole. They stepped back and fell down this hole.

3

4

'Don't Forget the Travelling Pills!!' by Philip (9) is an accomplished realisation of this pop-up story book form. He has an intuitive feeling for words and images, and both grow together on the page effortlessly.

➡️

Pop-up
(flat position)

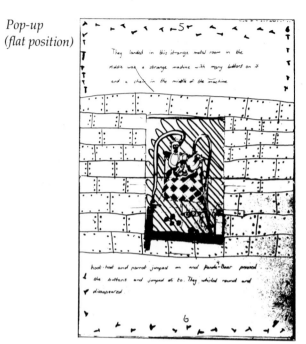

Philip uses the window on page 4 to see through to the North Pole on page 8, and the desert island on page 3 is seen through the windows on page 7. He exploits these dual images expressively by glueing a window frame to the negative pop-up space; one sees what is to be in the future and what has been in the past.

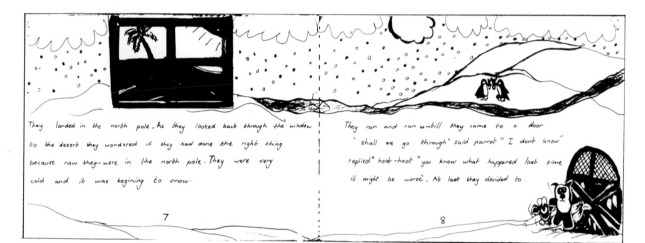

Door open

Flat pieces of paper made into environmental books are many in number. Two are described. The artwork and writing has to be done in the flat state so the positioning of rooms, inside and out, and placing of writing must be marked on the sheet before commencing work.

The design presents three inside and three outside walls of the room and four pages of writing.

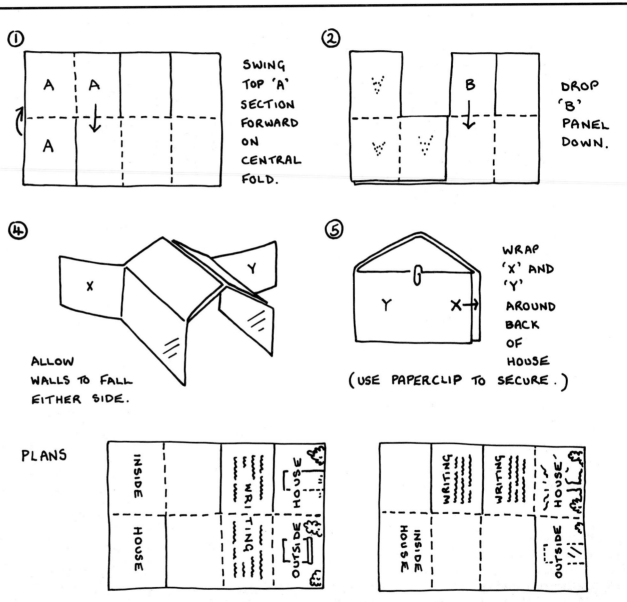

① SWING TOP 'A' SECTION FORWARD ON CENTRAL FOLD.

② DROP 'B' PANEL DOWN.

③ X LIFT ✳ TO CREATE ROOF Y

④ X Y
ALLOW WALLS TO FALL EITHER SIDE.

⑤ Y X→
WRAP 'X' AND 'Y' AROUND BACK OF HOUSE
(USE PAPERCLIP TO SECURE.)

PLANS

INSIDE HOUSE | WRITING | OUTSIDE HOUSE

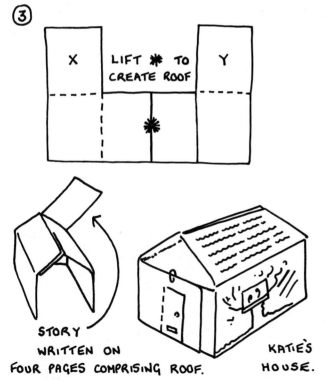

STORY WRITTEN ON FOUR PAGES COMPRISING ROOF.

KATIE'S HOUSE.

This method produces a three-dimensional theatre with five pages for writing/illustration on the rear panel.

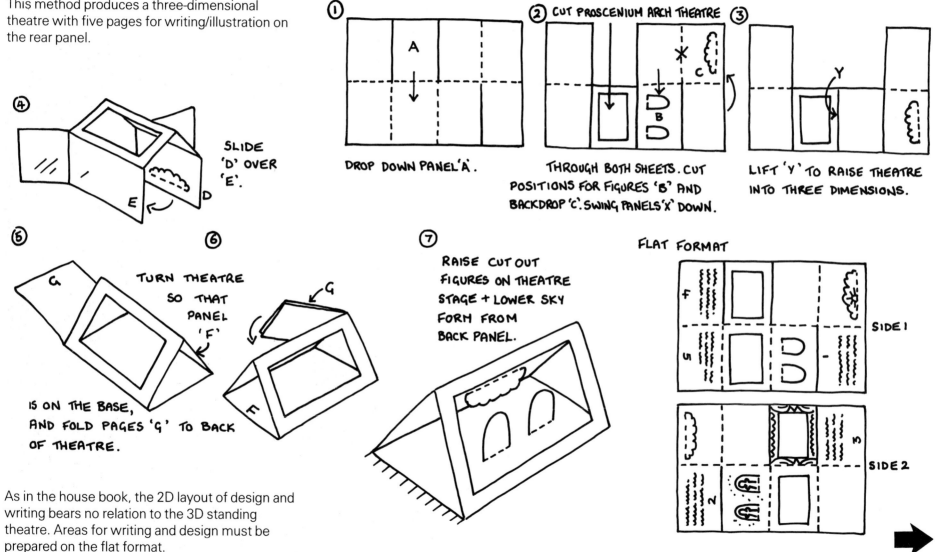

① DROP DOWN PANEL 'A'.

② CUT PROSCENIUM ARCH THEATRE THROUGH BOTH SHEETS. CUT POSITIONS FOR FIGURES 'B' AND BACKDROP 'C'. SWING PANELS 'X' DOWN.

③ LIFT 'Y' TO RAISE THEATRE INTO THREE DIMENSIONS.

④ SLIDE 'D' OVER 'E'.

⑤ TURN THEATRE SO THAT PANEL 'F' IS ON THE BASE, AND FOLD PAGES 'G' TO BACK OF THEATRE.

⑥

⑦ RAISE CUT OUT FIGURES ON THEATRE STAGE + LOWER SKY FORM FROM BACK PANEL.

FLAT FORMAT

SIDE 1

SIDE 2

As in the house book, the 2D layout of design and writing bears no relation to the 3D standing theatre. Areas for writing and design must be prepared on the flat format.

Nicola's 'Theatre Story' is a rhyming satire on Romeo and Juliet. Romeo is so small he has to stand on chairs, and Juliet is a kind of punk with bright pink hair. If they make a mistake a trap door opens beneath them, and they fall through to wild animals.

The scene through the proscenium arch shows the two performers on the raised (puppet) panels whilst the animals are drawn through the negative shapes on the base panel. The story on the five outer pages is carefully arranged on the page, and is balanced by the humourous accompanying drawings. Additionally, Nicola has added a moveable paper curtain to the front of the theatre.

'Theatre Story, by Nicola (10)

Rear-view presentation

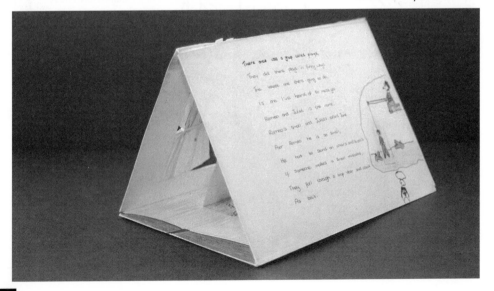

There once was a group called plays,
They did there plays in funny ways
The latest one there going to do,
Is one I've heard of so most you
Romeo and Juliet is the name,
Romeo's small and Juliet's called Jane
Poor Romeo he is so small,
He has to stand on chairs and stools
If someone makes a small mistake,
They fall through a trap door and used
As bait.

Concertina book with theatre

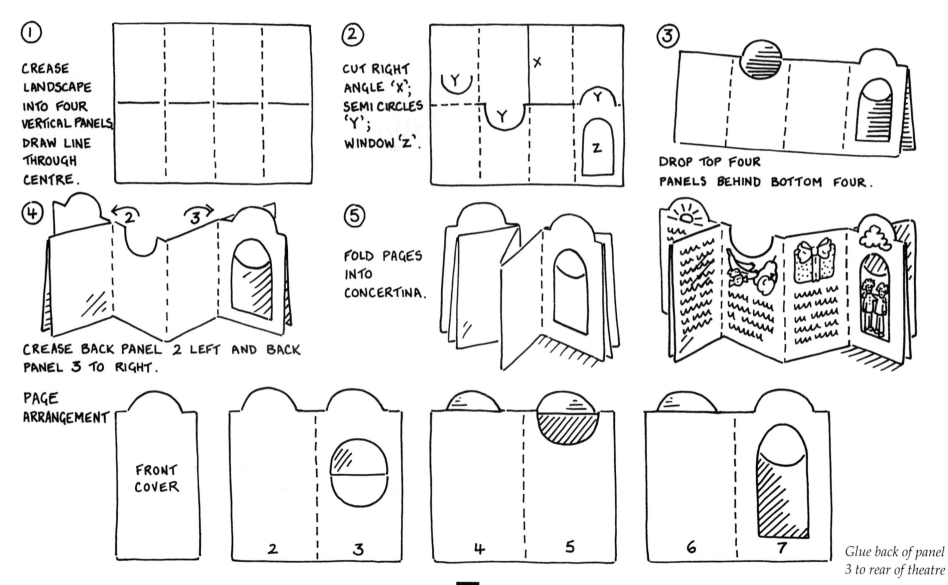

① CREASE LANDSCAPE INTO FOUR VERTICAL PANELS. DRAW LINE THROUGH CENTRE.

② CUT RIGHT ANGLE 'X'; SEMI CIRCLES 'Y'; WINDOW 'Z'.

③ DROP TOP FOUR PANELS BEHIND BOTTOM FOUR.

④ CREASE BACK PANEL 2 LEFT AND BACK PANEL 3 TO RIGHT.

⑤ FOLD PAGES INTO CONCERTINA.

PAGE ARRANGEMENT

FRONT COVER

2   3

4   5

6   7

Glue back of panel 3 to rear of theatre

The box

By Maimunah
Mumtaz

mum. Goldie "said Kate "Now go on, go to school Kate, you're going to be late." "Ok mum." Kate ran to school thinking about her new fish. She got to school very late. Why are you late?" Said her teacher. Kate didn't say any thing. "Go and sit down." Kate
4

sat down thinking about the fish. She wrote a story about her fish. Then the bell went for play time. Every one went out to play. Kate played with a skipping rope. It was time to go in to the class
. 5

room. She thought that the fish was flying. When she got home she saw that the fish wasn't in the tank. She looked in the box. She looked in the cupboard. She looked in the kitchen. Then she saw the fish flying across the kitchen roof and it dissappeared into the distance.
6

7.

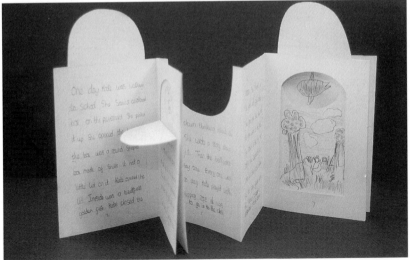

Cover and two spreads from The Box *by Maimunah (9)*

This is another story book which has been stimulated by a small box. After handling it and examining its contents, Maimunah wrote a story about Kate who finds a beautiful goldfish in a box. It turns out to be a flying fish who at the end of the story soars up into the sky and flies away.

The ingenious Flexigon exists in many forms and I am indebted to Edward Hutchins to whom I referred in the Introduction, who first revealed this particular one to me. Children are fascinated by the way the pages are secreted one inside the other.

CREASE SQUARE SHEET INTO SIXTEEN RECTANGLES. REMOVE FOUR PANELS.

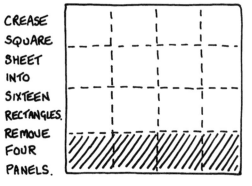

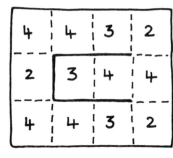

CUT HEAVY LINE AND NUMBER PAGES AS SHOWN.

① ASSEMBLY INSTRUCTIONS ② ③ ④ ⑤

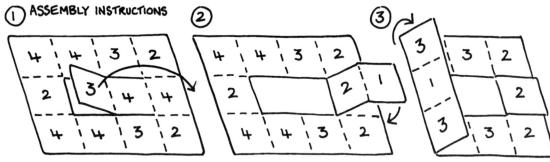

GLUE STRIP IN CENTRE.

⑥ OPERATING INSTRUCTIONS ⑦ ⑧ ⑨ ⑩

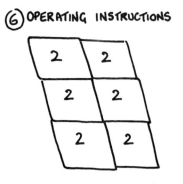

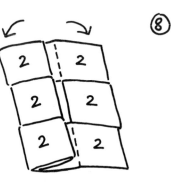

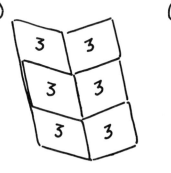

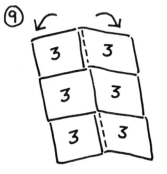

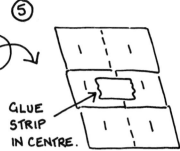

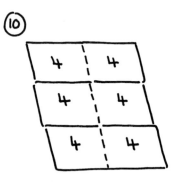

Grandma and Grandpa Monster by Kerry (8)

The three vertical panels of the flexigon is ideal for drawing people in a head, body and legs arrangement.

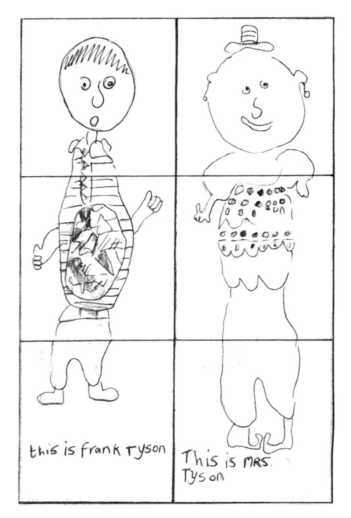

Famous people by Jody (5)

Telescope book 1

This is another book to come to me via Edward Hutchins. He once sent me a letter explaining in detail how the idea first originated with some friends of his on a car journey. It has become a favourite of mine (Why didn't I think of it!) and looks particularly effective if a range of coloured sheets of photocopier paper are used.

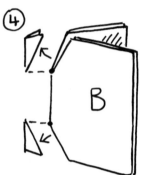

CREASE FOUR SHEETS OF PAPER IN HALF.

LAY TWO SHEETS 'A' TOGETHER AND CUT TRIANGLE FROM CENTRE OF SPINE.

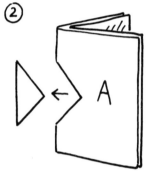

LAY 'A' ON TOP OF THE OTHER TWO SHEETS 'B' AND MARK TRIANGLE AREA.

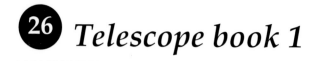

CUT WEDGES FROM TOP AND BOTTOM OF 'B'.

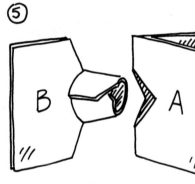

'TELESCOPE' RIGHT SIDE PAGES OF 'B' AND SLOT THROUGH HOLES OF 'A'.

LET RIGHT SIDE OF 'B' SPRING INTO PLACE ON RIGHT SIDE OF 'A'.

TO MAKE A COVER FOR THIS BOOK SEE INSTRUCTIONS ON PAGES 54 AND 55.

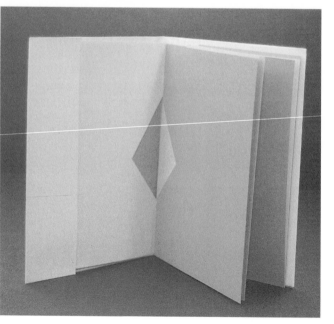

The pages in this telescope book are bound by an even simpler device than that described on the opposite page. Here linking pages are fed through a central slot. Even more care must be taken here in ensuring that creases are not made when curving the sheets into a cylinder and slotting them. Experiment with different kinds of paper and surface decoration – tissue, marbled paper, magazine 'collage' or wrapping papers. What kind of themes are most suited to this book form?

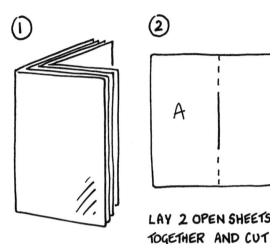

① CREASE FOUR SHEETS OF PAPER IN HALF.

② LAY 2 OPEN SHEETS 'A' TOGETHER AND CUT SLOT IN CENTRE.

③ LAY 'A' ON OPENED SHEETS 'B' AND MARK THROUGH SLOTS.

④ CUT TOP AND BOTTOM SLOTS ON 'B' LINED UP TO 'A' SLOT.

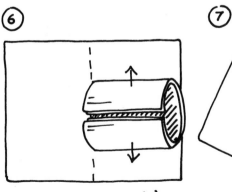

⑤ 'TELESCOPE' RIGHT PAGES OF 'B' AND SLOT THROUGH HOLE 'A'.

⑥ LET RIGHT PAGES OF 'B' SPRING INTO PLACE ON RIGHT SIDE OF 'A'.

⑦

Applied covers for books

1) Making a spine

This is an easy way to make a spine on a piece of paper or card. Make covers slightly larger than book pages to protect them.

2) Developmental covers

This cover uses the same technique as above but provides pockets for the first and last page to be tucked into. It is suitable for both concertina-type books and books which are stitched down the middle. The sheet of paper for the cover should be eight times the size of the single page, so if photocopy paper (A4) folded in half is used, this will need a cover sheet A2 in size.

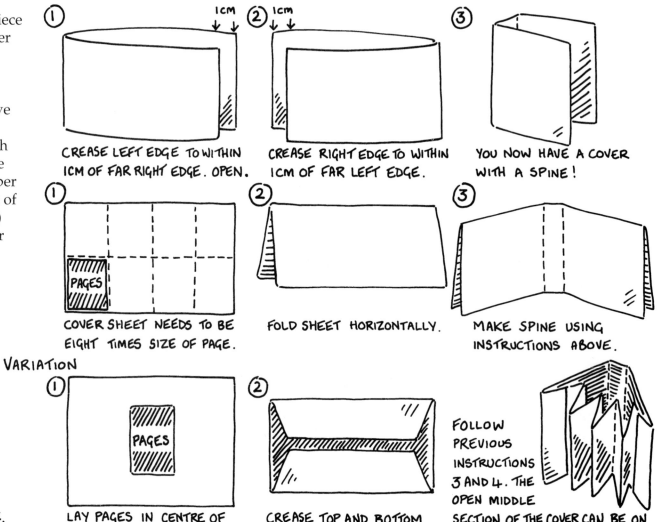

① CREASE LEFT EDGE TO WITHIN 1CM OF FAR RIGHT EDGE. OPEN.

② CREASE RIGHT EDGE TO WITHIN 1CM OF FAR LEFT EDGE.

③ YOU NOW HAVE A COVER WITH A SPINE!

① COVER SHEET NEEDS TO BE EIGHT TIMES SIZE OF PAGE.

② FOLD SHEET HORIZONTALLY.

③ MAKE SPINE USING INSTRUCTIONS ABOVE.

VARIATION

① LAY PAGES IN CENTRE OF COVER SHEET.

② CREASE TOP AND BOTTOM EDGES OF COVER OVER PAGES.

FOLLOW PREVIOUS INSTRUCTIONS 3 AND 4. THE OPEN MIDDLE SECTION OF THE COVER CAN BE ON THE IN, OR OUTSIDE OF THE COVER.

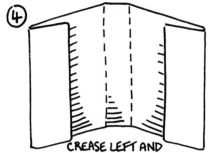

④ CREASE LEFT AND RIGHT EDGES INWARD TO WITHIN 1CM OF SPINE. TUCK BOOK PAGES INTO CREASED SECTIONS.

3) Basic cover (wrap around)

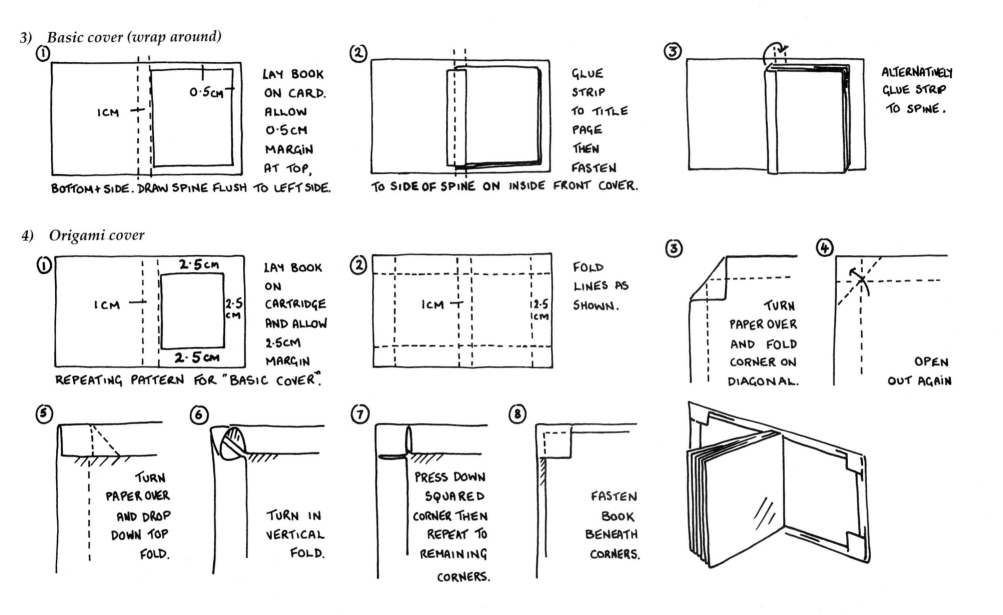

① LAY BOOK ON CARD. ALLOW 0·5CM MARGIN AT TOP, BOTTOM + SIDE. DRAW SPINE FLUSH TO LEFT SIDE.

ICM · 0.5CM

② GLUE STRIP TO TITLE PAGE THEN FASTEN TO SIDE OF SPINE ON INSIDE FRONT COVER.

③ ALTERNATIVELY GLUE STRIP TO SPINE.

4) Origami cover

① LAY BOOK ON CARTRIDGE AND ALLOW 2·5CM MARGIN REPEATING PATTERN FOR "BASIC COVER".

ICM · 2·5CM · 2.5 cm · 2·5CM

② FOLD LINES AS SHOWN.

ICM · 12.5 ICM

③ TURN PAPER OVER AND FOLD CORNER ON DIAGONAL.

④ OPEN OUT AGAIN

⑤ TURN PAPER OVER AND DROP DOWN TOP FOLD.

⑥ TURN IN VERTICAL FOLD.

⑦ PRESS DOWN SQUARED CORNER THEN REPEAT TO REMAINING CORNERS.

⑧ FASTEN BOOK BENEATH CORNERS.

Spine locks

Another way of joining pages into a cover is to use a spine lock. There are several variations of this type of binding and because it involves folding several sheets together it is best to use lightweight paper. To experiment with this form, start by creasing four sheets of photocopy paper in half and superimpose them one inside the other . . .

Version 2

The folding and cutting is the same as above. Then crease the top and bottom sections of the spine towards you, crease back again and project these sections to the inside of the book. To make these books more book-like, use a different thickness (weight) or colour of paper as the outer, cover page.

Version 3

The budding book artist can experiment with all kinds of spinal lock design. The cuts can go in the opposite direction, as shown, if wished; in fact one can pick and mix any of these horizontal and diagonal cuts to make different kinds of spinal pattern.

VERSION I.

 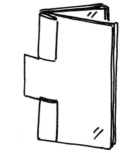

① CUT ABOUT 1CM THROUGH SPINE EDGE OF PAGES IN TWO PLACES AS SHOWN.

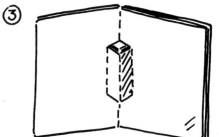

② CREASE MIDDLE SECTION OUTWARDS TOWARDS YOU.

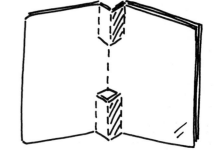

③ PUSH MIDDLE SECTION BACK AGAIN, OPEN TO MIDDLE OF PAGES AND PULL MIDDLE SECTION THROUGH.

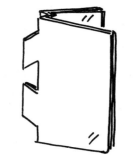

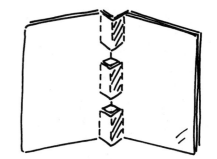

Locking methods

Pages can be held together by tying cotton thread over the centre fold of the sections that are creased inwards. Alternatively, a small twig or piece of folded paper the height of the book can be glued into the sections. There is also a rubber band locking method for books with a single middle section. Place the rubber band through the inside of the middle section, pull over the top of the book, down the outside of the spine and hook over the *top* of the middle section. Then repeat to the other end of the rubber band by pulling it under the spine and locking at the *bottom* of the middle section.

Non-stitched hard cover binding

Use the instructions on page 9 to make a concertina book. Then continue from here to give it a hard cover.

Self-portrait by Class 3 Hard covered concertina book with clasp

Nursery children working on individual pages of a group book. The pages were later bound into a hard covered book

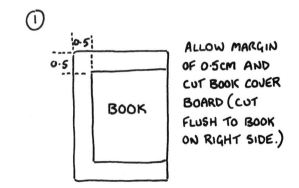

ALLOW MARGIN OF 0.5CM AND CUT BOOK COVER BOARD (CUT FLUSH TO BOOK ON RIGHT SIDE.)

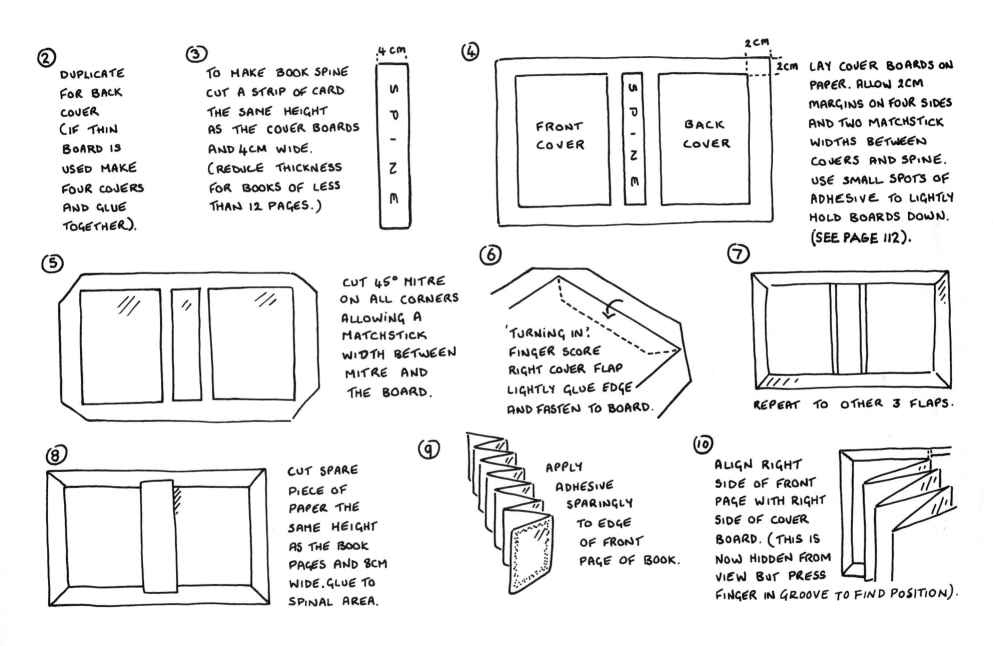

② DUPLICATE FOR BACK COVER (IF THIN BOARD IS USED MAKE FOUR COVERS AND GLUE TOGETHER).

③ TO MAKE BOOK SPINE CUT A STRIP OF CARD THE SAME HEIGHT AS THE COVER BOARDS AND 4CM WIDE. (REDUCE THICKNESS FOR BOOKS OF LESS THAN 12 PAGES.)

.4 CM.

SPINE

④ LAY COVER BOARDS ON PAPER. ALLOW 2CM MARGINS ON FOUR SIDES AND TWO MATCHSTICK WIDTHS BETWEEN COVERS AND SPINE. USE SMALL SPOTS OF ADHESIVE TO LIGHTLY HOLD BOARDS DOWN. (SEE PAGE 112).

2 CM

2 CM

FRONT COVER

SPINE

BACK COVER

⑤ CUT 45° MITRE ON ALL CORNERS ALLOWING A MATCHSTICK WIDTH BETWEEN MITRE AND THE BOARD.

⑥ 'TURNING IN'. FINGER SCORE RIGHT COVER FLAP LIGHTLY GLUE EDGE AND FASTEN TO BOARD.

⑦ REPEAT TO OTHER 3 FLAPS.

⑧ CUT SPARE PIECE OF PAPER THE SAME HEIGHT AS THE BOOK PAGES AND 8CM WIDE. GLUE TO SPINAL AREA.

⑨ APPLY ADHESIVE SPARINGLY TO EDGE OF FRONT PAGE OF BOOK.

⑩ ALIGN RIGHT SIDE OF FRONT PAGE WITH RIGHT SIDE OF COVER BOARD. (THIS IS NOW HIDDEN FROM VIEW BUT PRESS FINGER IN GROOVE TO FIND POSITION).

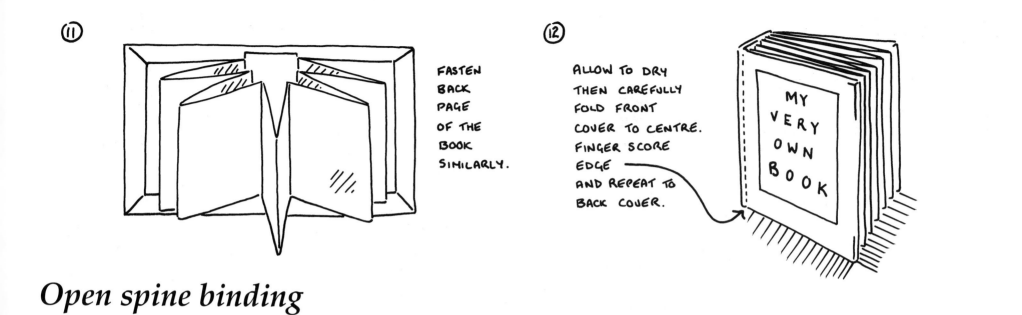

⑪ FASTEN
BACK
PAGE
OF THE
BOOK
SIMILARLY.

⑫ ALLOW TO DRY
THEN CAREFULLY
FOLD FRONT
COVER TO CENTRE.
FINGER SCORE
EDGE
AND REPEAT TO
BACK COVER.

MY
VERY
OWN
BOOK

Open spine binding

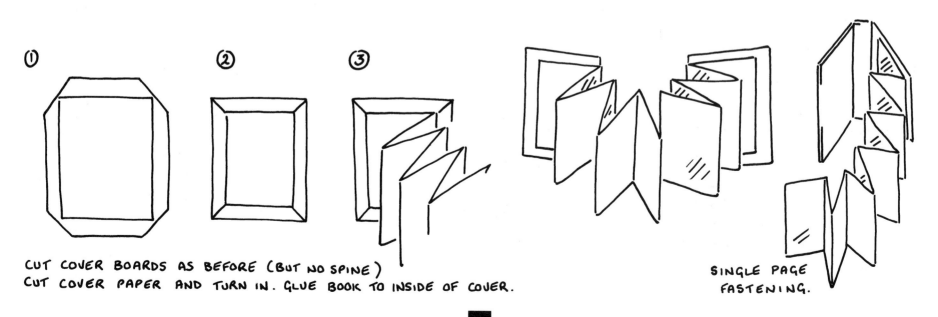

① ② ③

CUT COVER BOARDS AS BEFORE (BUT NO SPINE)
CUT COVER PAPER AND TURN IN. GLUE BOOK TO INSIDE OF COVER.

SINGLE PAGE
FASTENING.

Drafting books

One of the problems with preparing European, centrally-bound books is that one must calculate the number of pages required in advance of the book's assembly. To add pages to the back in order to continue a story also adds unwanted pages to the front. One of the ways to avoid this is to make a loose-leaf drafting book with slotted pages.

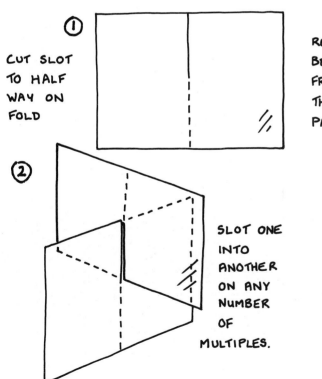

① CUT SLOT TO HALF WAY ON FOLD

② SLOT ONE INTO ANOTHER ON ANY NUMBER OF MULTIPLES.

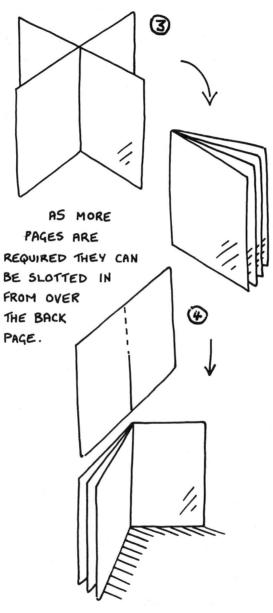

③

AS MORE PAGES ARE REQUIRED THEY CAN BE SLOTTED IN FROM OVER THE BACK PAGE.

④

General notes about folding paper

Folding sheets of paper too many times on top of one another can produce untidy creases. To avoid this the following folding pattern may be useful.

BASIC EIGHT DIVISION FOLD

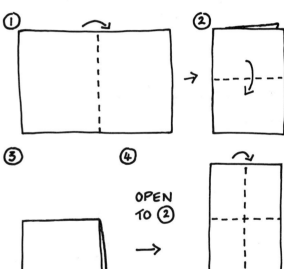

① ②

③ ④ OPEN TO ②

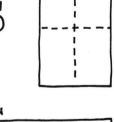

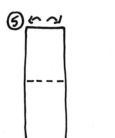

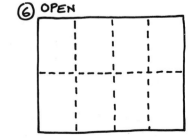

⑤ ⑥ OPEN

3 *Publishing in the classroom*

Looking at books

Even in the age of the CD-Rom and the Internet the main source of reading for pleasure and information comes from books. Yet it is so easy for children to take them for granted. They have to be reminded that for many children in the world there are no books. They are taken for granted in another way too. Does one contemplate the manufacturing technique, or design strategy of a book and how it conditions the decoding process as it is read? If the medium is the message, then to examine a book as an object is to add a new dimension to its meaning. Margaret Meek has been instrumental in revealing the 'multilayering' of the child's picture story book; that more is involved than solely the business of reading a text; that even very young children distinguish between different categories of print and are aware of the uses of space on the page and what the pictures 'say'.

When children make the whole book themselves from paper folding to 'cover to cover' content, they learn to communicate more effectively than probably by any other means.

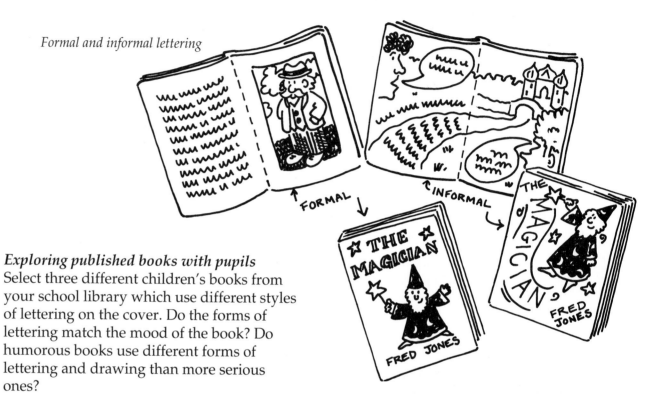

Formal and informal lettering

Exploring published books with pupils

Select three different children's books from your school library which use different styles of lettering on the cover. Do the forms of lettering match the mood of the book? Do humorous books use different forms of lettering and drawing than more serious ones?

Children learning to design their own books from using published books

The most common arrangement of book covers is: title, top; artwork, middle; and author's name, bottom. Select books which illustrate this arrangement as well as other layout patterns. For example, Author, top; title, beneath; artwork lower area of cover. Some book covers integrate the words into the artwork, and on others the words are down one side and the artwork on the other. Discuss these strategies with the class. Which ones do they prefer? In the book they are currently making which arrangement do they intend to use?

Other points when discussing published books:

- are the words too large or small on the cover?
- is the lettering on the spine of the book the same as the cover?
- does the cover illustration make you want to read the book?
- of the three selected books which one has the most compelling design? Can pupils explain why they think this is?

Discussion should also focus on the back cover and what publishers tend to put there, like the book's synopsis, publishers 'blurb', reviews, logo, bar code, price. Understanding the function of these categories not only introduces publishing methods, but how pupils can use them on the back covers of their own books.

BACK COVER COPY

Back cover 'copy'

Open the cover of one of the books you have selected. Compare the cover with the title page. Is the design different? Has the arrangement of words been changed? Adjacent to the title page is a page (or pages) with information like copyright, dedication and the address of the publisher called 'imprint page'. Pupils investigating these categories will see how they are necessary pieces of information before the book, as content, can begin.

One now enters the book proper – the beginning of the text. Picture book author/illustrators use so many different design strategies in placing words and pictures on the page that five books selected randomly from a library shelf would reveal as many different formats. Indeed, many authors use different arrangements from page to page hardly every repeating them. Uri Shulevitz (1985, *Writing with Pictures*, New York: Watson-Guptill) is one of the few writer/illustrators of children's books who has described at length how professionals do this. Although each page spread is seen as an individual design the whole book is envisaged as one boundless design. Shulevitz explains how he roughs out a picture book as if the pages are one continuous strip – like a Japanese screen painting. As he charts the book's layout design he can see climaxes in the visual design and contrast 'busy' areas (lots of things going on in a picture) with 'quiet' artwork that is more reflective in appearance; a book is a balance of highs and lows, of varying arrangements of words and pictures, and some pages will have no words, and some will have almost nothing on them at all. When the reader reaches the end of the book he or she should feel satisfied; not only has it been a good 'read' but the illustrations and overall design have enhanced and refined the experience.

If children can begin to look beyond the *content* of picture books and see the underlying *form*, it will help them when faced with the same challenge – holding the interest of a reader and communicating information clearly. There are many other aspects of book design and production that can illuminate the pupil's quest for expressing themselves through the book arts.

A visit to a local printer can show pupils at first hand how books are printed on large sheets which are then cut down into pages. Next the sections or 'signatures' are bound

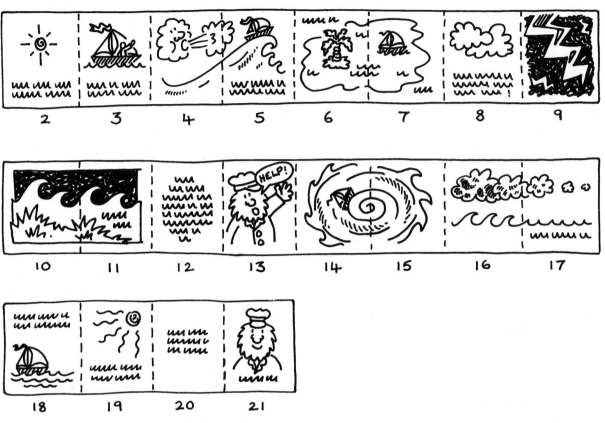

PLANNING A BOOK AS A CONTINUOUS DESIGN.

VARIATIONS OF LAYOUT PLANS.

together by another department or separate bindery. Seeing the colour separation process in reproducing artwork demonstrates how colour pictures are made up of individually printed 'layers' of colour. In the classroom pupils can then simulate this process by superimposing washes of colour using transparent paint or pencil crayon to make a picture. If a professional illustrator visits your school pupils can find out how book illustrations are made and what materials are used. Very often it is the simplest of techniques like pencil crayon that are the most popular with the professionals. Pupils can make illustrations in the same way.

Writing to be read

There is ample evidence to show that pupils write best when what they produce is to be read by others. Writing for a specified audience gives a reason for doing it. 'Publishing', in the classroom context, has come to mean the stage at which pupils externalise their writing – present it to a real or imagined audience.

For all but the youngest writers a published text must be relatively free of errors; it must receive a seal of editorial approval if others are to read it. Handwritten or word processed texts and visual material assembled in a folder, mounted sheets of work presented on a display board, a stapled leaflet, or hard-bound book are all publishing strategies.

However, publishing in the book art

context differs from professional publishing – not so much in *what* is published, but *how* it is presented. We have seen that professional children's writers and illustrators expend much energy on determining just how the story as words and the story as pictures are unfolded in a book.

Books are usually made in thirty-two page 'sections'. But an average picture-story book of twenty-four pages will provide the author with ten or so page spreads after title page and imprint have been accounted for. Thus the word and picture narrative must fit into a set number of pages. This does not necessarily mean that each of the available pages has a different episode of the story because some pages may be given over entirely to illustrating a part of one episode. But broadly speaking that is what happens – each page records a sequence of the story. Clearly, if children can organise writing in the same episodic way, much of the confusion so commonly found in their narratives can be avoided.

Thinking in a book way helps pupils to develop:

- the ability to plan a text episodically – each page spread should contain a section of the story/category of information
- the skill to select words economically, so that they 'fit' the available page space
- the adroitness to organise what is to be communicated in words and what in pictures

Graphic frame

- the visual dexterity to design a page spread

Chapter 1 looked at some of the design strategies commonly used by book designers. Some pupils, even quite young ones, will intuitively place words and images on the page satisfyingly. Others will need guidance. A useful strategy is to use a graphic frame which provides areas for writing and areas for illustration. Try making one or two yourself in black line work like the one shown.

Then photocopy them for the class. These are used either as drafting sheets (after editing, the work is transferred to a book form) or, particularly with younger pupils, used as the finished presentation (glued into a concertina book). In time, pupils will be able to prepare their work without using these sheets. If you can illustrate the graphic frames with examples from published books, it will make the experience more meaningful.

Book launching
Celebrate the publication by distributing a limited edition of each 'title' as follows:

- one book for the 'school collection'
- one for the pupil's assessment folder
- one for the pupil to take home

Preparing the pages
The appearance of self-made books will be improved if the writing and artwork are contained within templated borders. If it is appropriate for pupils to draft their work they should draw round a template in the centre of their drafting book pages. Drafting is then done in precisely the same area as the finished book, and editing notes can be made in the area around the template border.

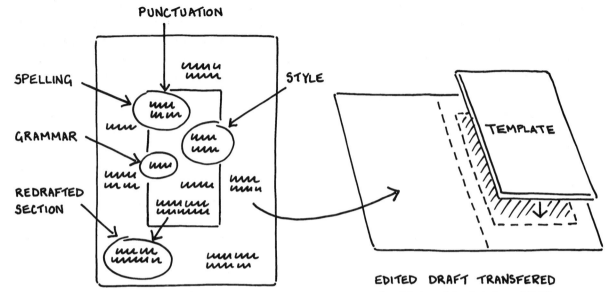

Using templates to draft and present work

EDITED DRAFT TRANSFERED TO SAME TEMPLATED AREA IN BOOK.

Printing and assembling
A good size of paper to make books from is 210 mm × 297 mm (A3). Children are often surprised to see that in most basic books the top four panels are upside down to the bottom four panels. When a book is ready for publishing lay an opened sheet on a photocopier and reduce to half size (A4). Make a limited edition of each pupil's work – say three/four copies. Is it possible for pupils to learn to operate the photocopier themselves and fold, cut and refold copies down into the prescribed book form?

Other ways of publishing
The growing number and sophistication of computers in school has inspired desk top published newspapers and magazines. More directly, pupils write by hand or word process pieces of information of interest to the school community and 'paste up' the copy on base pages. These can then be photocopy-published using the same method as above.

Another publishing approach, especially where the publication is to run into several pages, is to prepare it on a standard format (for example landscape A4) with the centre fold stapled. The children of Brookburn Primary School in Manchester used this method in publishing *A Piece of Chorlton* – a study of the shops in their local high street, Beech Road.

Researching and organising

The class of ten year-olds responsible for making this book walked up and down Beech Road with a clipboard and made a list of the shops and commercial premises. Two parents and a student teacher accompanied them and supervised the visit. Each pair approached a different shop and asked the shopkeeper/owner if they could return the following week and interview them for a book they wanted to write about the street. There was a very positive response. Returning to school, pupils now designed a questionnaire: what did the shop/business sell and who owned it? How long had it been there? Was there anything special about it, or unusual about what was made or sold? Did the shopkeeper/owner have any anecdotes to tell about customers?

The pupils then returned to their appointed shop, carried out their survey and took notes. Before returning to school, drawings were made of either the exterior or interior of the shop, or some special feature of it like an object in the window.

At the next session the format the book would take was shown to the class. Twelve sheets of photocopying paper (A4) were folded in half. A thin piece of card the same size as the paper was folded as a cover and both pages and cover were stapled together using a long-arm stapler. The leaves each had two pages and two sides making a total of four pages per sheet. This provided forty-eight pages. Three pages were designated as title page and other preliminary pages, so this left forty-five pages to be divided between the twenty-four shops in the survey. It was pointed out that extra leaves could be inserted into the book if required.

The brief was for each pair to have a page spread for their shop. Layout patterns were suggested on the board so pupils had a broad idea about how to present their material. The pairs discussed what pieces of information collected on the questionnaire were the most interesting. They each folded a sheet of photocopying paper in half and drew around a card page template. Pupil 1 started to draft the text for the spread, and pupil 2 made a drawing or diagram to accompany it.

By the third session ideas had been exchanged and redrafting set in motion; the artwork was well under way. Towards the end of this period attention was drawn to the appearance of the text/artwork on the spread. If it was to be handwritten could a particular style of writing reflect the business in question? If word processed, a time had to be allotted to pupils to use the one computer in the classroom. Pupils found that fitting a picture into an appointed space is much easier than fitting words into a space. So it was logical for the space required for the writing to dictate the zone for the artwork. During this design-oriented time pupils looked at magazines and discussed with the class teacher how texture, pattern and different kinds of drawing techniques and ways of presenting the 'copy' were used by professional magazine designers.

This was a mixed ability class so basic writing skills varied enormously, but it was essential that every pupil should feel involved in the project and be helped to make his/her page visually interesting. During this time it was found that some shops required more than two pages, and others needed only one. It was also found that one extra page was necessary to complete the book. As all pages were to be photocopied the final copy/artwork had to be worked over with black pen.

Researching

Preparing the questionnaire

Completing the survey

Designing copy and illustrations

Preparing for photocopying

Photocopying

Assembling

Launching

Pagination and assembly

Later in this book I discuss the problem with preparing a book in which all pages are laid one inside the other and bound. By the end of the fourth session this became an issue. We had nearly all the individual pieces of work to be included in the book completed. But what order were they to go in? We discussed how a butcher's shop could contrast with a book shop, and that the Post Office, requiring three pages, would need a single page entry to follow it.

Once the order had been decided came the process of pagination. We returned to the 'mock-up' and numbered the pages from 1 to 48. When the pages are removed from the book and seen separately, the page sequence of course changes. For example, page 40 faces page 7, and 32 faces 17. So while the whole book has to be conceived in its chronological form the arrangement of pages for photocopying is completely different to that. The pages of the restapled mock-up were labelled with the relevant shop. Pages 1 and 2 the Butcher's; page 3 and 4 the Book Shop, and so on. The staple was removed from the mock up, the leaves separated and the original copy (including title page, an introduction, acknowledgements and contents page) glued to the relevant pages. To create

consistency of design one pupil was asked to write all the page numbers in. Finally two pupils designed the cover.

A Piece of Chorlton was published in a first edition of one hundred copies. Each page spread was photocopied on both sides × 100. The cover was printed likewise. Then a 'conveyor belt' system of pupils and staff paginated the piles of individual sheets (checking that they were in the right order) and finally they were stapled together. The grand launch took place in the book shop on Beech Road, attended by many of the local people and of course the children who had made the compilation.

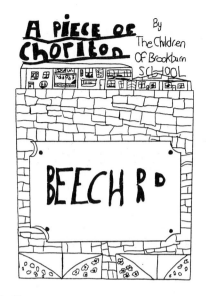

 1 *Cover*

 title page

Following the practice of published books, pupils have made the design of the title page different to that of the cover

2 *The classical format of left page text, right page illustration. The decorative border sets the writing off nicely. Had this been done around the illustration it could have looked fussy*

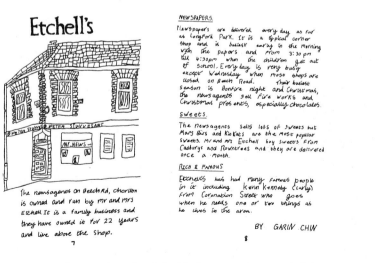

3 *The arrangement of artwork and sub-headed text makes a satisfying asymmetrical design of five rectangles*

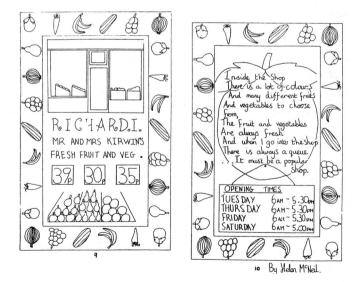

4 *This spread is delightfully pleasing to the eye – lettering, handwriting and carefully drawn thematic images all combine into a total design*

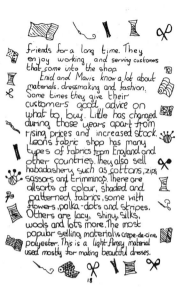

1 Lighthearted cartoon-style graphic representation of 'De Lambolle Coiffeur'

2 A more carefully arranged cartoon-inspired design

3 The text about a building and heating specialist has been skilfully arranged in the shape of a drop of water

4 Freely arranged border using objects associated with fabric

5 Objects associated with the chemist's shop have been integrated into the textual area

6 'Embarrassing moments in the Delicatessen.' Effective balance of text and illustration on one page

7 Solely visual representation of a grocer's shop showing where in the world the goods come from

8 Word-processed poem with computer generated border design reflecting the card shop merchandise

④ *Multicultural and special needs focus*

The fundamental book ideas expressed here have their origins in South-east Asia. Does the simplicity of the origami book have something to teach our 'advanced' technological society, in which if there is a computer 'virus' whole industrial and commercial complexes fail to function?

Books are universal forms, as relevant for children in Finland as Jamaica. So are the heroic stories of folklore inside them, that seal a nation's cultural identity. Can any child not be enthralled by the legendary tales of Rama and Sita from India, or the stories that have grown around the African honey bird?

The National Writing Project did much to encourage family literacy especially amongst those families for whom English is not the home language. Whereas pupils writing in a language other than English have tended to be traditionally discouraged, there is evidence that a growing number of schools are designing programmes aimed at pupils writing bilingually. To value and build on children's home language is more likely to produce a good command of standard English from them than to ignore or reject it.

Gatehouse Books in Manchester have specialised in involving Somali parents and their children in writing both in Somalian and English. Seeing their writing in print has boosted their self-confidence and stimulated a real desire to communicate information about themselves, their ideas and feelings. It is not unusual to find teachers of Chinese brush painting and calligraphy, and Japanese teachers of origami, visiting our schools to teach these fine crafts. When these skills are related to calligraphy and painting in the European tradition, and realised in the basic book form, the young communicator is crossing the cultural history of the world to make a social as well as personal statement.

The Clever Woman and the Dancing Bear, Gatehouse Books

'*Maryam told the story in Somali, and Affi helped to translate it into English. Sian wrote it down. Suad and Shokri drew the illustrations'. It is a story about a woman who dressed in men's clothing to go shopping because the bear who might attack her only eats women. She meets the bear and they dance. Finally men come and kill the bear. Those involved with this publication said on the fly leaf: "We like the story because the woman is very clever. We like the dancing. If you read our story you might be frightened, or you might laugh. You might cry at the end".'*

One dark quiet night Fred the Ted was reading a story in bed. Suddenly he heard a noise. Tap. Tap. Tap. It was footsteps!

Fred's Scary Night by Class 1B

Illustrated by
Nadia Atcha, Sohail Musa, Mehreen Patel, Adam Rubbani, Samira Pandor, Eazaz Puda

The Honey Bird by Amina (10)

Amina, who comes from Pakistan, has retold the traditional African story of the honey bird. She has drafted her text so that it fits the side panels of the book form perfectly.

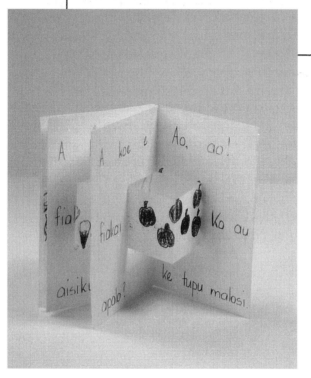

Toku Fiakaiga by Timei Pedro (10)

Timeo made, wrote and illustrated this pop-up origami book in his school in the Solomon Islands.

Cover and spread from Fred's Scary Night

Scary Night was improvised by a class of seven year-olds whose second language is English, and then illustrated in the book form by individual pupils. The book was then reproduced by colour laser and the pages laminated to protect them. This book now has an honoured place in the school library.

Special needs

Jan, a teacher who has spent most of her teaching career with special needs pupils, uses basic book forms extensively in her work. She argues that most pupils with learning disabilities are only too aware of their disability and often feel socially detached from other children because of it. She sees building confidence in her pupils as her prime role: without that no effective learning can take place. Jan finds holding forms for writing like the exercise book intimidating for her pupils. She sometimes uses small format notebooks in an attempt to make writing more amenable, and to reduce the stress of what she calls the 'overwhelming challenge of putting marks on paper'. But it was attending an INSET course in the book arts that made her begin to experiment with paper folding as a holding form for writing.

The first books she made for ten year-old special needs pupils to work in were a disaster. 'I spent all weekend making ambitious pop-up books. I took them in on Monday morning full of expectation and excitement, but the pupils rejected them because they said they were too "difficult". I was very disappointed.' On reflection she deduced from the experience that the rejection was triggered by the unfamiliarity of the form. Pop-ups were just too much to take in. So she made much simpler books – the origami kind – and these proved to be much more successful. There were no 'fancy bits' to distract or confuse, just three page spreads and small format ones at that. Jan, eager not to make the task too challenging, made no reference to these books being like 'real' published books but rather as fun things you could write in. 'Even to call them books could have sent shock waves through some pupils,' said Jan. 'How one approaches even the most basic forms of writing like recording how many brothers or sisters you have is crucial. At times with older pupils their level of emotional development makes them prone to reject almost anything you try to involve them with.'

Over a period of several weeks these book forms were used on several occasions so that pupils would become familiar with them. Very gradually Jan aimed for more committed work and found to her delight that some pupils returned to the same book even after an interval of days. With one particular group she had never experienced this – each lesson had had to be designed as a 'one-off', so no development work had been possible. As confidence in writing grew Jan returned to the pop-up books she had originally made, and found that now there was a very different attitude to them. Pupils who had been reluctant to draw now drew pictures on the pop-up forms and this led to the construction of simple written narratives beneath them. Moreover, pupils began to see that these books were similar to published pop-up books they were shown. At first they were somewhat taken aback by this, but as the notion that they were making books like printed ones sank in, Jan became aware of a sense of pride in their work.

What was also of significance at this stage was that for the first time pupils wanted to share their work with each other. Normally this would have been unlikely to happen because writing was regarded as a labour – something that had to be got through. It wasn't so much that what was written was uninteresting, but that the act of writing made it so. Books were passed around the table and read, or pupils held their books and told the story or explained the theme work inside them. Increasingly pupils wanted Jan to help them with spelling and word forming. And because only a few sentences are necessary to fill an origami book, this was never a Herculean task. 'It was thrilling for me when they asked if they could take their books home,' said Jan. 'I had never been asked this before after any other piece of writing they had done.'

With another teacher, Andrea, who works with much younger children with emotional and physical disabilities, it was the intimacy of these books that made them so valuable. One particular pupil, Oshawi, would not speak at all and all attempts failed at involving her with activities like group play and games, but she could be persuaded to play in the sand providing other children were not there too, and she would draw with crayons sometimes too. It was through this tactile involvement that Andrea decided to leave some small basic books lying around near where Oshawi was sitting and to see whether she would respond to them.

At first she ignored them but then her

My Family by a special needs pupil

curiosity got the better of her and she picked one up. The next day the books were in the same place and this time Oshawi went directly to them and handled them. Nearby were some crayons and before long Oshawi was making marks in them. She carried the book around with her for the rest of the day and took it home with her. Andrea felt that this gesture was an important milestone in Oshawi's development and that much of her subsequent progress could be traced back to it.

Books with infants

Building up a relationship with young children is essential to their developing the self-assurance to write. Beryl teaches a mixed reception/middle infant class and has done just that by using children's self-made books.

The first book she made with them was a simple folded card with door (these are illustrated on page 15). The children loved these because of the element of surprise and simplicity. She finds the concept of writing a strain for many children. A way around this is to encourage scribble writing to gain

confidence in the pencil and this helps to avoid the break in thought processes which so easily happens when young children start to write. The books Beryl made for them were so exciting to look at that their fear was overcome. In standard writing books they feel compelled to write on and on as if psychologically programmed to 'finish the book'. This is a daunting prospect and turns children off writing. With one-off books the teacher can decide what kind of book and what length of book is most suitable for each child.

From the simple folded card developed the

basic origami book (see page 20). The children were encouraged to draw first so that their illustrations would be a further stimulation to writing. As Beryl says:

> 'Children need to orally communicate their stories without fear of writing expectation by the teacher.'

From the six page origami book evolved the concertina book (see page 9), with its four large format pages.

The children found these exciting, but they still needed to be 'eased' into them from the smaller books they had just finished. To

Contour book by Lindsey (5)

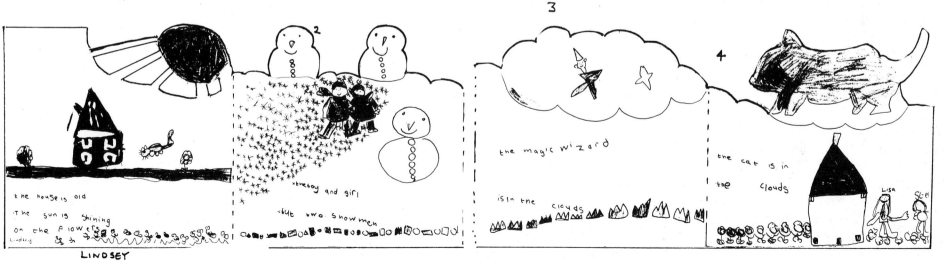

achieve this Beryl designed a cut contour to the four pages. In the first books these were very recognisable shapes. For example, Lindsey's book had:

– sun with rays
– head and shoulder
– cloud
– cat

Lindsey wrote:
(1) the house is old the sun is shining on the flowers

(2) the boy and girl but (sic) two snowmen

(3) the magic wizard is in the clouds

(4) the cat is in the clouds.

With Leeanne's prescribed contours the figuration was less defined as shown below.

Beryl thinks children generally don't enjoy writing:

'They get lost in standard writing books, but their own books make writing enjoyable. Parents can't believe what they've done, and children can't wait to make the next one.'

Leeanne wrote:

(1) Once upon a time there was a magic hill the hill stole all the colours of the rainbow one day the magic hill was ill

(2) the towns never heard about the hill one day the hill went out for a walk the magic hill saw a ghost the hill spoke to the ghost

(3) the hill said who are you the ghost

 = HILL

 = TOWN

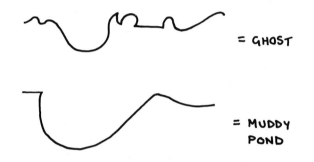 = GHOST

= MUDDY POND

Leeanne (5)

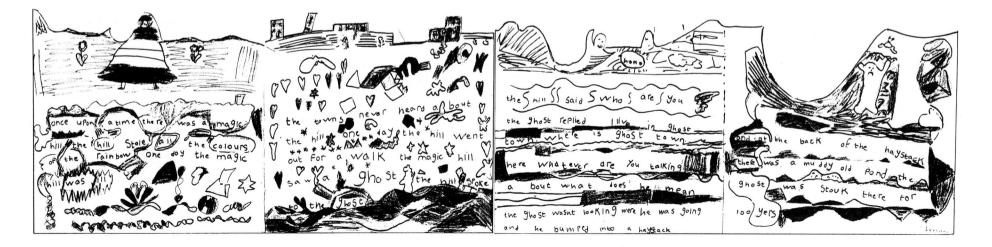

replied I live in ghost town where is ghost town here whatever are you talking about what does he mean the ghost wasn't looking were he was going and he bumped into a haystack

(4) and at the back of the haystack there was a muddy old pond the ghost was stuck there for 100 years

There is much greater confidence in (*a*) the story structure, (*b*) writing, (*c*) artwork, (*d*) total page design. The whole book is a visual delight, an explosion of shapes and colours.

There was a tendency for each panel to be completed in its entirety before moving on to the next one. Children would come to Beryl and seek guidance and reassurance before progessing.

Jennifer's book has vague outlines but by this stage of making books the ability to interpret a shape has advanced.

'and one day they were playing out. One of them said to the other come and play in my house and she had a basket it was brown and it had a black handle with yellow pins . . .'

Between these examples is Mary's in which stars, staircase and windows are clearly delineated by the teacher, but the child has

Jennifer (6)

and one day they [   ] were Playing out. one of them [   ] said to the other come and Play in my house and She had a basket it was brown and it had a black handle with yellow Pins. She has Purple wallPaper and then her mum was Shouting up to them she was saying to them can you go to the shop and get some food for me we have got no food So they got basket and set off to the shop they were very quick and they got all of the stuff in the basket.

When they went to the shops there mum said they could get Something for them seif and they got some greeps and they did not see a noet that Said magic greeps if you eat the greeps you can make a' wish and when they got home they found out that they were magic greeps and they did see the note and they did eat the greeps very quick and they did wish to be twins and oll of a sudden they were twins.

Mary (6)

it was night and the stars shining but three stars were different one was purple one was red and one was pink

but below the stars there was a field in the field a house was there in the house lived a farmer the farmer had a boy the boy was caild Sam Sam was looking out of the windoW he sawthe 3 stars he wet up the stairs he took his Bag and rushed down and went out

out side on the hill he opened his bag he took out a ladder The ladder went right up to the stars he took the stars and went home

and had tea with his dad alfer a while Sam showed his dad the 3 stars and his dad took them and yousd them to make 3 decorations

extracted more than a basic concept from them.

Lisa's book represents the cut contour technique at its most challenging and productive, for her story covers the eight pages. The shapes correspond to four pages of story matched on the reverse. In each of the pages Lisa has visualised a different situation. The cellar window of page 2 is the centre of the flower of page 7. Descending stairs page 3 – ascending stairs page 6. Three windows of page 4 become trees on page 5.

Another way of continuing the story but without turning the page was invented by Steve (6) who, when reaching page 4

Lisa (6)

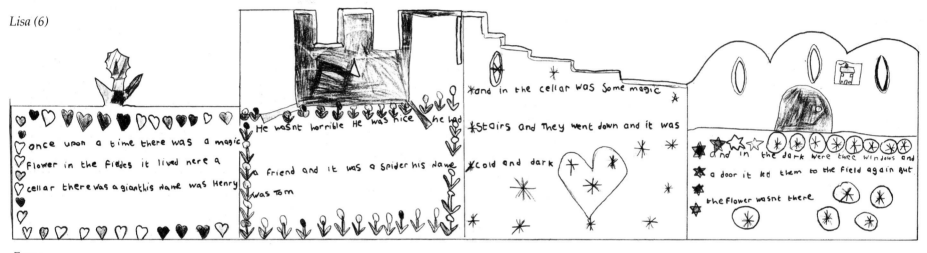

Front

Once upon a time there was a magic flower in the fieldes it lived nere a cellar there was a gian this name was Henry

He wasnt horrible He was nice he had a friend and it was a spider his name was Tom

and in the cellar was some magic stairs and they went down and it was cold and dark

and in the dark were three windows and a door it led them to the field again but the flower wasnt there

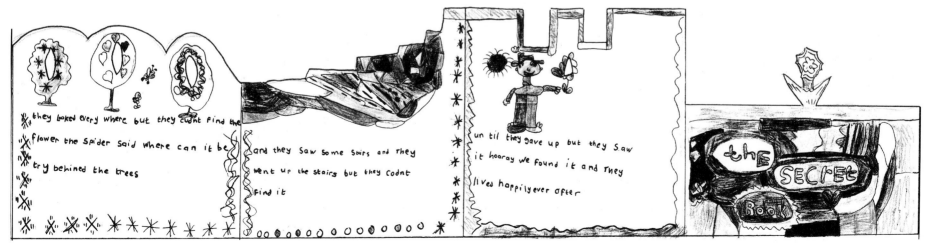

Back

they looked every where but they cudnt find the flower the spider said where can it be try behined the trees

and they saw some stairs and they went up the stairs but they codnt find it

un til they gave up but they saw it hooray we found it and they lives happily ever after

the SECRET Book

78

continued the story in an attached origami book.

All these books evolved through the stimulus of the concertina form itself. Without the book and its outlines it is questionable if so much developmental writing would have occurred for, as Beryl said, 'the outline is an aid to discovery'. Beryl's visual aid shows children how cut shapes can tell a story.

'The Two Flying Cars' by Steve (6) illustrates, again, the intuitive sense of design that children have if free to express it in an atmosphere conducive to creativity. The words and images coexist in perfect asymetrical harmony on the page. This book was made on good quality, heavy cartridge paper, and Steve has reciprocated quality of paper with quality of work. Could anything like this have been produced in a tatty exercise book? The reward for so much effort was for Beryl to bind the book using hard covers which Steve ultimately furnished with a cover design.

Finally, two side-bound books. (For details of this technique see p.103.)

'The Castle Book' by Rachel (5) is an illustrated story in six pages and in 'The Butterfly Book, by Lisa (5) the illustrations and text have been made on separate pieces of paper and glued in. This is an excellent approach for children who need to write 'as the spirit moves them' without the prescription of a set number of pages. For the

Steve (6)–Page 4 showing origami book on bottom right side of page

IMPROVISATION TECHNIQUE SHOWING BRAINSTORMING RESPONSES.

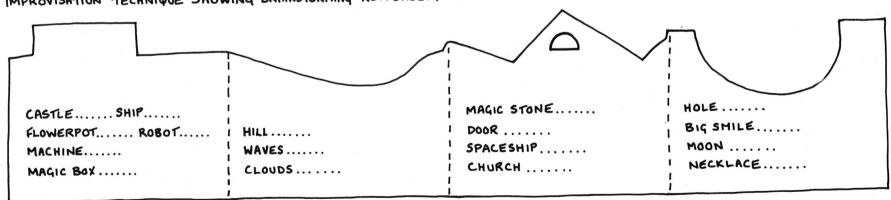

CASTLE......SHIP......
FLOWERPOT......ROBOT......
MACHINE......
MAGIC BOX......

HILL......
WAVES......
CLOUDS......

MAGIC STONE......
DOOR......
SPACESHIP......
CHURCH......

HOLE......
BIG SMILE......
MOON......
NECKLACE......

BERYL'S VISUAL AID SHOWS CHILDREN HOW CUT SHAPES CAN TELL A STORY.

THE TWO FLYING CARS

THE Two Flying cars

by Steve oliver
illustrator Steve oliver

author and illustrator

BROADHEATH

One day the two flying cars went on a trip

they went to Blakpool and they bought some candy floss

then they went to Pee balis and they played in the balls

when they had finished they went to bed in the mornig they bought a hat each

and at night they went to see the illuminations and it was good

and then they had tea and it was egg and bacon chips and then the went home and to bed

less confident child the artwork and writing glued down one piece at a time is a stepping-stone process, building confidence in writing. Later, Lisa was confident enough to make a whole book working directly on to the paper. (Both books were bound by the class teacher.)

These few examples show how an imaginative teacher can build confidence in writing skills through the concrete stimulation of the book form.

'The Castle Book' by Rachel (5)

'The Butterfly Book' by Lisa (5)

Books in the nursery

These books by four-year-olds illustrate how the concertina fold presentation can enable even very young children to sequence their thinking and image making.

Jacqueline's 'the cat is sitting down' (picture 1) is a simple one-fold form showing imagery on all four surfaces.

In Heather's book (picture 2), the four-phase sequence shows (*a*) Heather; (*b*) her Mummy and Daddy; (*c*) having tea – milk jug; (*d*) teapot (a 'flowered' teapot).

David's 'story' (picture 3) shows (*d*) 'me'; (*b*) 'taking a doggy for a walk'. It is interesting to observe that although there is perceived a chronological sequence, it does not necessarily move in a left to right direction.

Sacha said of his story (picture 4) 'This is a man going for a walk through some trees and he sees a monster who chases him.'

This three-sequence story (picture 5), produced on a single origami book structure, shows clearly how the prescribed form has projected a forward development of imagery. From (*a*) isolated house, to (*b*) house with garden, to (*c*) 'me standing by my house'.

Finally, Samantha's retelling of Goldilocks (picture 6) sequences the story for her in a visually controlled evolution of images.

Nursery children at work on their books

①

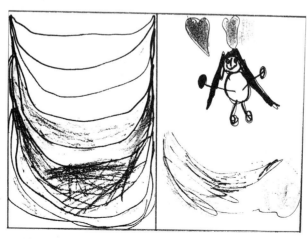

Cover

Inside

②

a   b   c   d

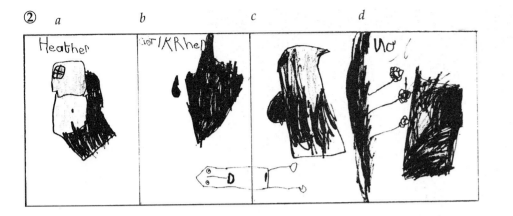

③

a   b   c   d

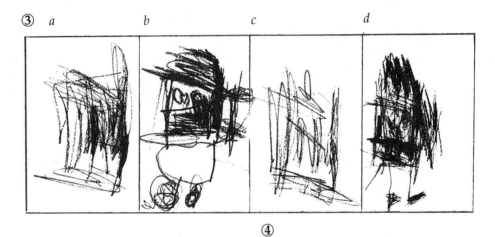

④

⑤ a   this is my house

b   these are the flowers in my garden

c   this is me standing by my house

⑥ once upon a time there was a girl called goldilocks

and this is where she lived

and this is the three bears house

this is the woods

6 A book of many styles

This book concept was the result of a project with thirty-two year four pupils. The aim was to develop several different writing styles incorporated into one collective book. It was divided into eight parts for no other reason than that it fitted equally into the class size. In practice, the distribution of eight tasks was not rigidly adhered to, some pupils preferring alternative strategies.

The objective was to use the story form as the catalyst for styles of writing not normally associated with fiction but which, nevertheless, fitted strategically into it. The synopsis of the prescribed story was as follows:

A child sees a poster advertising an exhibition of a valuable object. On visiting the exhibition the child sees thieves steal the object. A newspaper reports the theft. The gallery offers a reward. The child writes to the gallery to report what he saw. This is announced over the radio as a newsflash. The child remembers a vital clue to the thieves' identities and whereabouts. They are arrested. The child uses the reward money to have a holiday.

The division of activities:

The extra activities required to complete the book were done by members of each group as they completed initial work. This was sometimes a joint effort.

Classroom tables were rearranged to accommodate groups of eight and an object placed in the centre. These objects were brought from home and comprised various pieces of valueless objets d'art. They were colourful, small, but large enough for everyone in the group to see clearly. Some children had writing or artwork only roles, whilst others had joint writing/design roles. The visual work was of three kinds: (*i*) observational, based on the objects; (*ii*) imaginative, illustrative, pertaining to the story; (*iii*) layout, design tasks.

Task description

1 *Poster design*   This involved selecting information appropriate to the exhibition. Brevity was essential. Artwork of precious object an important part of the design, as was total arrangement of words and images on page.
2 *Story Part I*   From child seeing poster to witnessing theft.

3 *Newspaper article*   Headline caption, reported account of theft.
4 *Reward poster*   Similar to 1, selecting relevant information, artwork, design.
5 *Letter and envelope*   Child writes to gallery explaining what he/she saw. Design of envelope, stamp, franking.
6 *Broadcast newsflash*   TV/radio reports Police now have a clue to identity of thieves.
7 *Story Part II*   Child remembers vital clue which takes him/her to a local shop where thieves are. Reports this to police. Thieves arrested.
8 *Illustration for 7 above*   These last two roles are inter-changeable. Extra writing/ illustration could be added if necessary.

Extra tasks

9 *Postcard*   Child sends postcard home from holiday. Side A, picture of holiday. Side B, message home. Stamp, franking. Task for one or two children working on either side of postcard. (Two sheets glued together if working in pairs.)
10 *Title page*   Design of title, author, artwork.
11 *Cover*   Title design and artwork – strip for spine title.
12 *Synopsis*   Written precis of story as book page advertisement for book. Copyright information, date of publication.

Blackboard diagram

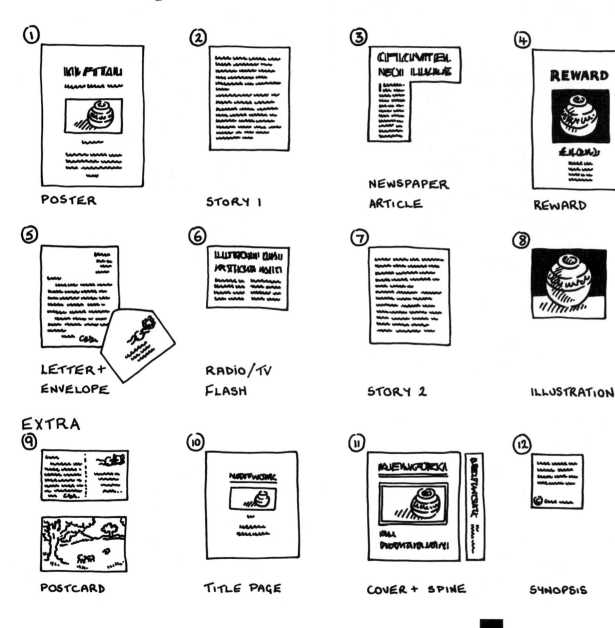

① POSTER

② STORY 1

③ NEWSPAPER ARTICLE

④ REWARD

⑤ LETTER + ENVELOPE

⑥ RADIO/TV FLASH

⑦ STORY 2

⑧ ILLUSTRATION

EXTRA

⑨ POSTCARD

⑩ TITLE PAGE

⑪ COVER + SPINE

⑫ SYNOPSIS

As a stimulus I showed the class *The Jolly Postman* by Janet and Allan Ahlberg (Heinemann, 1986), a delightfully original storybook including lift-out letters throughout. I had explained to them the basic eight-part story structure, with visual references made to the blackboard diagram. A brainstorming episode explained various ways in which the precious object could be stolen, who stole it, how the thieves could be traced, what clues they left behind and how they might be apprehended. Defining the precious object required another improvisation period. The blanks for finished work were distributed to the 4 × 8 children groups.

1 and 4 – comprised A3 cartridge paper.
2 and 7 – paper for story (slightly smaller than A4).
3 – newspaper article in right-angled shape. Horizontal top for headline caption, bottom rectangle for article.
5 – A4 letter and ready-made envelope
6 – paper for newsflash.
8 – cartridge square (15 cm) for illustration.

Postcard – large postcard format, 10–12 prepared similarly from cartridge.

(All the above sizes were designed to fit the proportions of the A2 (3 × 2) book pages.)

These blanks were placed in front of them as aids to visualising the task. Rough paper for writing, design and artwork drafting was also provided along with art materials – a range of pens, crayons, pencil crayons.

Group discussion was encouraged. For example, the name of the object had to be agreed before most participants could commence drafting. The story I (picture 2) was crucial to newspaper article (picture 3), and the revelations of the letter (picture 5) conditioned the newsflash (picture 6), story II (picture 7), and the illustration (picture 8).

The drafting process also had to take into account the shape and size of the master blanks. Too few words would leave an empty space; too many words wouldn't fit.

Towards the end of the first drafting period, the groups read their work (or showed illustrations) to the rest. This enabled the cohesion of the contrasting styles to be tested. Some rewriting became necessary at this stage.

Some of the tasks required special skills, for example poster, reward designs, letter writing and envelope addressing format. For this purpose visual aids were prepared which indicated these requirements. The drafting and collaborative process enabled all the children in the group to experience writing and design styles other than their own. This was important otherwise each child would only have become familiar with one style of writing presentation. An alternative strategy to this group method, and one appropriate to older children, would be for each child to make their own book of many styles of writing.

The task of the final presentation of work on the master blanks was the major activity for

① Exhibition poster

② Story 1

the second part of the project. Those who finished first moved on to tasks 9–12. The completed work was housed in a book designed to accommodate them. This was done by cutting slots on folded pages through which the material could be slotted (1, 3, 4, 5, 9). And uncut pages were prepared for glued-down work (2, 6, 7, 8, 10, 11).

The reader can imagine the fun and excitement of 'journeying' through the book – taking out folded posters, reading newspaper articles and postcards, opening envelopes. It is not surprising that the whole class asked if they could start a new one right away!

STOLEN MULTI-COLOURED LIQUORICE

On Wednesday 24th May in between 12 and 1 p.m. two people, a man and a woman escaped out of the Whitworth Art Gallery with the Ancient Multi-Coloured Liquorice made by the egyptions. If you think you can describe these people please contact Whitworth Art Gallery or phone 483-6056

③ *Newspaper article*

Reward

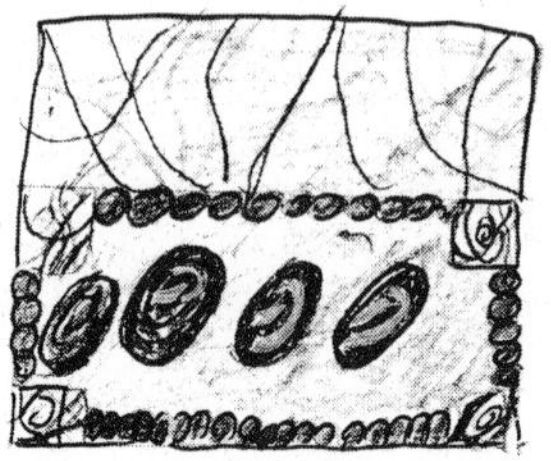

Whitworth Art Gallery offers £ 100,000 pounds for the recovery of the ancient egyptians multi coloured Liquorice. If you have seen it call 483456

④ *Reward poster*

3 Adria road
Didsbury
Manchester
M 20 0SQ
24th May 89

Dear Director,
I saw a man and a woman take the multicoloured liquorice. Between 12.00am and 1.00pm. They put it in a sweet shop bag. I followed them and they saw me. But I know where they are.
yours Faithfully
Tom Farra
P.S. I will tell where they are.

⑤ *Letter and envelope*

89
24 May
3 Adria Rd.

The Director
Whitworth Art Gallery
oxford rd
Manchester.

BBC NEWS

We interrupt tonights exciting ball game to bring you further commentary on the theft of some ancient valuable liquorice from Witworth Art Gallery in Manchester. The liquance made by the ancient Egyptians has achieved its different colours by juices from assorted trees in Egypt. It was layed in a jeweled case and forgotten about for hundreds of years. It was found in the coffin of king Zilk and is worth £100,000. Just today witcworth had a letter from a boy called Tom Farra saying that he saw two people steal the ancient multi coloured liqolice and has helped the police enormously with their enquiries. So thankyou Tom and thankyou for watching BBC News

goodbye.

⑥ *Radio/TV newsflash*

Tom was trying to remember what the man and the woman had with them. they had a bag with them but he couldn't remember what it had on the bag. He crossed the road and saw a sweet shop. It was Charlies sweet shop. then he rembered the man and the wom an were holding a bag with Charlies sweet shop on it. He ran into the shop and saw the man and woman with the stolen oldcck he sprinted down the street to the nearest phone box and dialed 999. About 5 minutes later he heard the siren. He looked down the road and saw the police car. He shouted at the police to stop their car. So they stopied the car, arrested the theives and gave Tom £100,000 and Tom went on Holiday.

⑦ *Story 2*

⑧ *Illustration*

Dear Mum and Dad

I'm having a brill time in Crete. Its absolutely scorching The hotel that I am staying in has an outdoor swimming pool I have had a swim in it once. It is lovely. The food is delicious especialy the wine. I have met a boy called Jack.W have been exploring together.
I am looking forward to seeing you.

Lots of Love From

Tom xx

P.S. The sun has made me really brown.

Mr & Mrs Farra

3 Adria Road
Didsbury
Manchester M20 0SQ

ENGLAND

⑨ *Postcard*

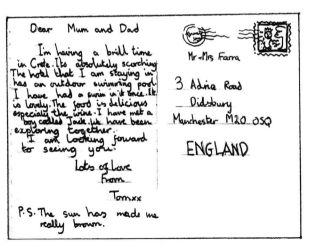

10 *Title page*

11 *Cover*

12 *Back page/cover synopsis*

Book format

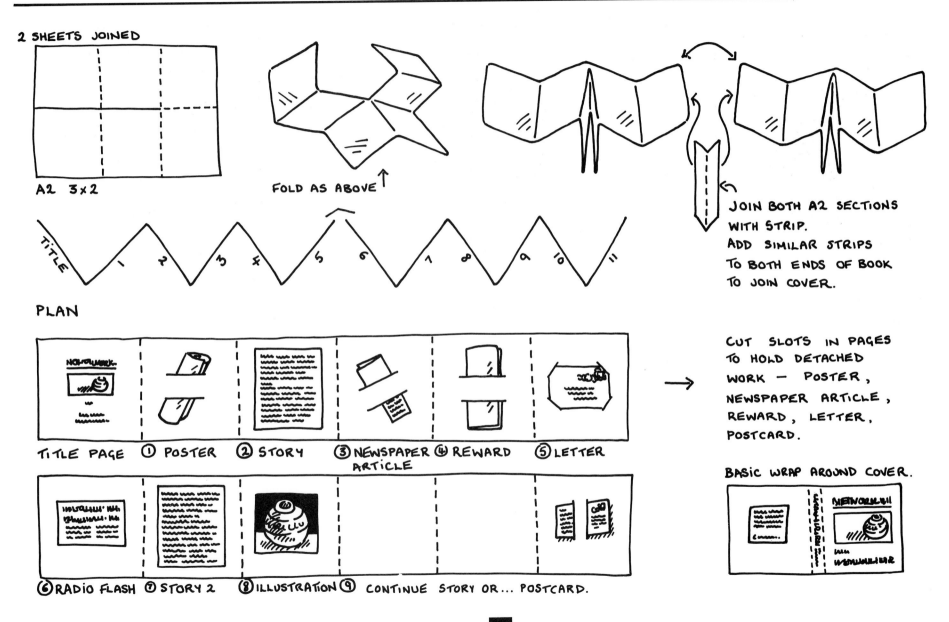

2 SHEETS JOINED

A2 3 × 2

FOLD AS ABOVE ↑

JOIN BOTH A2 SECTIONS
WITH STRIP.
ADD SIMILAR STRIPS
TO BOTH ENDS OF BOOK
TO JOIN COVER.

TITLE 1 2 3 4 5 6 7 8 9 10 11

PLAN

TITLE PAGE ① POSTER ② STORY ③ NEWSPAPER ARTICLE ④ REWARD ⑤ LETTER

CUT SLOTS IN PAGES
TO HOLD DETACHED
WORK — POSTER,
NEWSPAPER ARTICLE,
REWARD, LETTER,
POSTCARD.

BASIC WRAP AROUND COVER.

⑥ RADIO FLASH ⑦ STORY 2 ⑧ ILLUSTRATION ⑨ CONTINUE STORY OR... POSTCARD.

Fastening book to cover

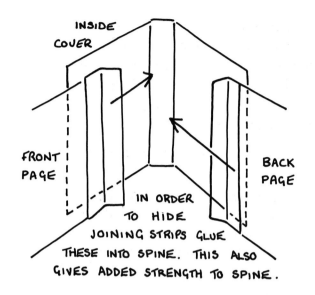

INSIDE COVER

FRONT PAGE

BACK PAGE

IN ORDER TO HIDE JOINING STRIPS GLUE THESE INTO SPINE. THIS ALSO GIVES ADDED STRENGTH TO SPINE.

Crystal Palace

by Class 2L

Palace of Peking

by Class 2L

The Mystery of the Disappearing Gobbstoppers

By Class 2L

During a visit to Queen's Road Primary School I met Gwen, who teaches Class 10 – a mixed five and six year junior class – and she took me across the playground to her mobile classroom. The small space was packed with children in school uniform and Gwen had asked them to make display labels with their names on, placed on the tables so that I could address them personally. After a brief introduction, during which I showed them different kinds of children's illustrated books, I turned to my ritualistic improvised story. It went something like this:

(Give me an object) A square (A square what?) A box (Can someone give me a rectangle?) A brick. (Now what's different about this brick?) It's soft. (And its colour?) Pink. (So we have a soft brick. Who owns it?) Mark (What did he do with it?) He threw it through a school window. (A soft brick through a window?) It was soft glass. (Then something amazing happened to the brick – what was it?) It was taken aboard Concorde. (I want this story to be more interesting than just an ordinary Concorde . . .) A special interplanetary concorde. (And how does this fit with the soft pink brick in the classroom?) This superhuman concorde was collecting all the soft bricks of the world and taking them to another planet called Redegon. (And what about Mark?) He was taken too. (How did he

get back?) By specially propelled parachute. (Where did it land?) In Africa. (Can we make something extraordinary happen here?) A strange kind of giraffe carried Mark and the soft brick to the Mediterranean. (Oh, I see Mark brought a pink brick with him. And next?) A subterranean creature with diamond false teeth took Mark and the brick to Greece – and then he went to Italy. (Now wait a minute. How did he get to Italy if he didn't have any money?) He sold the creature's diamond teeth to buy an air ticket – then over Europe by hovercraft – then under the English Channel, where Mark found the surface of the sea frozen over – so he put on propeller boots with metal studs and twisted himself like a drill till he reached the surface – then up the M1 in a modern car with wings which took off near Birmingham and brought him home . . . (What about the brick?) He found it tasted so nice – like strawberry ice cream – that he ate it.

This warming-up process, opening up doors into, and out of, the subconscious, and the oiling of the imagination laid the foundation for the morning's work. This was to make a composite, illustrated storybook.

Before we began I requested rough books at the ready and explained that as soon as they had 'invented' part of the story they were to write it down. Unless this was done they could forget their contribution. We then

brainstormed a theme: hat, elephant, rocket, cat and the class settled for a small box. Working in sequence, from child to child I navigated the story around the room.

The Snuff Box

Philip sat nearest the window so he began our story:

> 'A man is walking along with a snuff box in his pocket and he takes the snuff box, opens it, and puts some snuff in his nose, and he drops the snuff box and loses it in the grass.'

Seea continued:

> 'A midget comes along and finds the small box. He empties the snuff and puts some magic potion in it.'

The story then changed hands thirty more times; sometimes becoming repetitive, at other times stereotyped. Nevertheless it continued, held together by an ever-changing central focus. At moments where the lateral thinking seemed to be taking an obtuse direction I tried to steer it back again as unobtrusively as possible. This was particularly true as the story neared completion when I reminded the last four contributors that they had to bring the story to a close. A precis of the story would be something like this:

'A man drops a snuff box and loses it but it is found by a midget who replaces the snuff with a magic potion. Someone finds the potion and turns into a frog. A wizard's cat eats the frog and turns bright green. Then a spider eats the wizard. The spider which has become enormous falls down a grid in the road but climbs up again into a passing car. The family in the car visit an insectarium where the spider is declared a rare species. Growing gigantic again, the spider eventually reaches New York and climbs the Empire State Building. It falls off, demolishing buildings in the process, but the police eventually catch it and it turns back to its normal size. A man is walking along a path and he sees a small box . . .'

A rather unsynchronised story but standard for a first attempt.

The next stage was to distribute A4 paper and for pupils to draw a 2 cm margin down the left side on the horizontal format; this was to be the binding edge of the completed book when bound. The illustrated books shown earlier were produced again so the children could see how a storybook page can be designed; the text can be wrapped around illustrations; words and pictures balanced, often asymetrically to produce a satisfying aesthetic unity. I drew some graphic layouts on the board showing approaches to page design: they had to ask themselves which part of their story sequence was most important and needed the most pronounced visual image on the page. If it were too small or poorly positioned it would fail to focus the attention of the eye; if it predominated too much it would fail to attract prolonged attention. The picture 'filled out' the story and revealed information the words could not provide. For example, the background scenario presented an environment which the words did not describe.

After the rough sketches which determined the relationship between text and illustrations, the class set to sketching out the page in light pencil. Horizontal lines indicated the placing of lines of words, and basic outlines suggested the placing of drawn objects. (Part of the brief was to include their names as part of the design.) From here they were free to continue as they wished. It was easier to fit the illustrations around the words than vice versa, so I suggested that the text should precede the artwork. One final point I made to the class was that I intended to photocopy the finished book so that strong linear work was preferable to light pencil work. The problem with this kind of suggestion is that children then think they have to put a thick black line around everything. They tend to do this at the best of times and my instructions were hardly designed to counteract the habit. I tried to help them to see how the main characteristics of a perceived object is rarely its outline but more likely what lies *inside* the form. I did two quick sketches on the board in an attempt to illustrate my point: one of a head and the other of a fireplace. Then I drew a thick black line round both pictures to show how it destroyed the logic of the free line image. All this was done in a few seconds and then rubbed off before anyone could start incorporating either image into their work. Teachers know that once an image, in any subject or media, is shown to a class it becomes instantaneously a model to be adopted. How one stimulates without indoctrinating children is one of the major concerns of teaching.

By this time we were half-way through the morning and so had just over an hour to develop the book page. The class worked quickly and I darted around the room checking the story line for mistakes before it was finally 'written in'. (In fact several children slipped through the net and there are some spelling and grammatical howlers in the collection.) The artwork developed at varying paces. The first person to say 'I've finished' was, if I agreed with him or her, commissioned to design the book cover. Often the pupils would declare that the work was completed but on inspection more could have been done to reap success. I don't think 'filling in' the empty spaces necessarily enhances or broadens a drawing's appeal. The converse is often true.

Philip's design (picture 1) contains only a schematic sun as background to the figure and tree and the strength to these images ensures

⑤ The man who was turned into a frog dropped the box. Then a wizard came along and because he was a wizard he knew exactly what the potion was

ROGER BRITISH

⑥ The Wizard came along and saw the cat with the frog in his throat and the cat turned bright green

Vicky Lennon.

⑦ The Wizard turned really small. The cat put his tongue out and got the frog out

⑧ And then the wizard could not turn back. Then a spider came along and ate the wizard up.

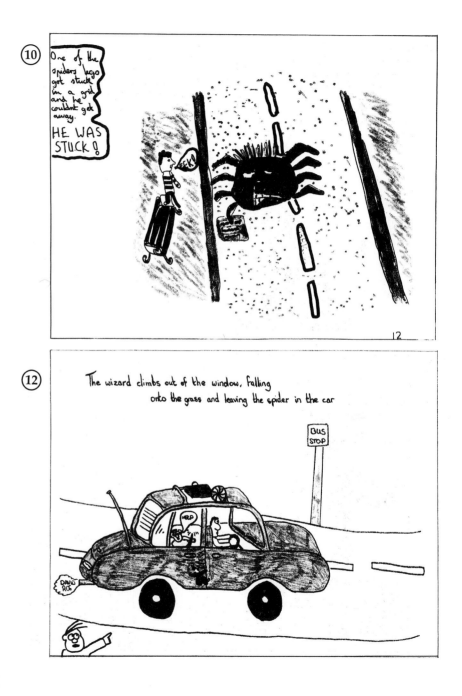

13 Fred and his family go to the insectarium and the spider crawls onto his shoulder. They reach the insectarium and the attendant saw it and said it was a rare species.

INSECTARIUM

ENTRANCE

PAUL MITTEN

ADMISSION
CHILDREN £1
ADULTS £2
O.A.R's £1

14 The spider gets put into a box, which used to belong to the dwarf and it has got a magic potion in it. And the spider grows to the size of Mount Everest.

MAGIC POTION

HELP

15 The Spider got out of the box and went down a grill. He travled for thousands of miles and came up in New York and climbed up the Eempire State building

Gareth

Blakeley

16 About one hundred men came down the street carrying something very long and then one of the men said, "I think this leg belongs to you."

ANTHONY HO...

that it is in no sense an 'empty' composition. This is even more true of Magnus' layout (picture 17). The two figures are so consistently and confidently drawn in a graphic, sharp-edge style that anything else would have made the composition cluttered. We shall return to Magnus later, because with David (picture 12), it was clear that I had two budding graphic artists here. On one of my later teaching visits Magnus brought me his folder of drawings to show me. At ten he not only had a well-formed personal language of

drawing, but he could articulate verbally what he was doing and intending to do.

The artwork varies from the over-simple (picture 2) to the over-complex (picture 11). Visual skills can lie several conceptual years apart. Iain (picture 8) draws everything without perspective from a front and side viewpoint. Whilst Mark (picture 9) makes a brave attempt at perspective and forshortening. Andrew (picture 14) became so engrossed in the spider drawing, concentrating on the minute detail of the facial

features that the rest of the page was ignored. Gareth (picture 15) conveys a very powerful central spider image, intensified by carefully drawn classical architecture.

There is probably greater consistency in verbal fluency than artwork but this is to be expected considering the emphasis on writing in the curriculum. What concerns me most here is not so much the indigenous standards of the verbal and visual material, but how they coexist on the picture plane.

The writing in picture 7 fits uncomfortably with the tree's branches, but Jannine (picture 3) makes a pleasing composition of juxtaposed words and images. In picture 2 both forms of communication stand well apart and unrelated but picture 17, whilst holding the two idioms apart, makes a visually satisfying composition. Perhaps Paul's (picture 13) is one of the most successful pieces. Here the words and clouds dance a polyphonic pattern and contrast with the solid building in the foreground. Vicky (pictue 6), still harnessed to the schematic sun and tree form, portrays the wizard and cat with a natural harmony. The total design holds the page well.

A week later I was able to deliver three bound copies of 'The Snuff Box' to Class 10, side-bound in yellow silk thread. No stimulus, however awe-inspiring, could have eclipsed the motivating effect that these books produced on the group. When I said 'For our next book . . .' I knew by the unremitting enthusiasm that greeted my words that these children, like me, were hooked on books.

Strictly speaking, I had deviated from the classical Japanese side-binding technique in binding 'The Snuff Box', for I had bound single, not folded leaves. The next project, however, was to make a more formal approach to the oriental art.

Side-bound story books

I had bought my first side-bound book only two years previously in a bookshop in Berkeley, California. It was P'u Ming's *Oxherding Pictures and Verses* translated from the classical Chinese by Red Pine. I showed this to the class, displaying how the writing and illustration lived in perfect harmony together; and later I took the book around the room (it was too delicate to be passed round) so they could see the beautifully textured rice paper from which the book was made.

Traditionally, Japanese four-hole binding is a style in which stitches are made at four points. Sometimes binding occurs in five holes (which is the Korean style) but in China, where preference for even numbers is culturally endemic, four-hole binding has been the order for centuries.

I explained to the class that in oriental binding the leaves are folded in half and then paginated separately (not one inside the other as in European bookbinding) with the fold on the outside, and the open ends of the folded sheet on the inside 'spine' of the book. There is no actual spinal strip to support the pages for, unlike Western books which place

tremendous tension down the centre spine, in oriental binding the tension is more evenly distributed *across* the spinal area. Another characteristic I wanted the children to observe was that the covers of my side-bound book were bound in the same manner as the pages inside and were, indeed, of much the same quality of paper (not thick paper as in Western paperbacks).

Perhaps the greatest advantage of the Japanese book is the organisational flexibility of its contents. With European bookbinding the number of pages to accommodate a 'one-off' story must be calculated before the final book writing can begin. The total number of words must be divided by the average number of words per book page; space for illustrations added to that; then pages added for title and end pages, before the number of pages required for the whole book can be drawn up and the writing begun. With side-binding no such elaborate planning is necessary. The formation of the book is simplicity itself; the pages following on one independently from the other, require nothing more than the author to construct the contents of the book in the same page-at-a-time manner. One simply adds pages as one goes along. If a page is spoilt in some way then it is replaced.

It was now time to embark on the pupil's own personal side-bound books, using the experience of group story making gained from the previous week's session. An A4 sheet of white paper had been divided into two A5

sections. The left section was ruled with lines, and the right left blank. About two hundred of these were duplicated, providing, I thought, enough leaves for everyone in the class. When folded, these sheets formed a writing right leaf and, on the reverse, a plain side for illustrations.

The class was then shown how a book of single sheets would be made. I produced a simulated book, completed with four-hole binding, and with this image of the book firmly planted in their minds I set to the story stimulation.

I brainstormed, not a theme, but the first few words of the story. Out of the many titles three were put to the vote:

1 In the middle of the night
2 It was lying there beside the path
3 As the water got higher

Number 2 won. I made a few suggestions: keep the story moving, introduce people, places and things when you feel the story needs it; aim for a climax of some kind and a resolution. I wanted them to imagine themselves as writers, writing and illustrating a book for children younger than themselves. This gave an added incentive for making the book and concentrated their minds on holding the interest of a reader. Stories were completed in draft and exchanged for 'proof-reading' (children are perhaps the most astute critics of literature!). The final version was started on the prepared paper. Pages were to be numbered centre bottom or top. (This avoided the possibility of numbering on the outer corners and thus losing the numbers in the binding.)

Children were at liberty to either write the story then illustrate, or to illustrate as they went along. It was a challenge to scan the written page and extract from it the essence of that part of the story for visual treatment. It is in tasks like this that the need to make a visual image energises the imagination. It is not simply illustrating a particular incident in a story, it is being faced with an unprecedented sequence of ideas which by accident of lines of writing come together as a page. It was from these chance relationships that a coherent picture image had to be composed. In the recorded interviews with children which follow, these kinds of problems, amongst others, are expressed.

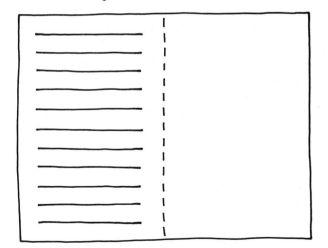

A4 horizontal format – left A5 lined for written work, right A5 left blank for art/graphic work

'It was Yellow with Blue Spots' (*Catherine*)

Q What were you thinking about as you started the story?

A I wanted to make it interesting. I was trying to think about who might be reading the story.

'The Bowler Hat' (*Sarah*)

'My story is about a boy who finds a hat so he takes it home and in the morning he finds a man in it. The man says that to save the world he has to find a special flower hidden down a tunnel at the back of his garden. So the boy goes in search of it.'

Q Were there problems with matching the page of writing to an illustration?

A There wasn't always much happening that I could illustrate so I had to search in the story for something I could draw. I like reading science fiction and Agatha Christie. They gave me ideas of how to put a story together.

'The Buttermoth' (*Magnus*)

'I'd been doing some drawings and so I based my story on one of them. I decided I wanted it to be amusing and not serious. Some ideas came easily and some I had to think about a lot.

The story is about a monster who was found by the side of the road by another group of monsters. They wanted to brainwash it so that it would tell them where the really evil monster was.'

Q Did they succeed?

A No!

Q Drawing is something important to you, isn't it?

A Yes. I had the illustrations in my sketchbook at home and so I decided to use them for my story.

Q So you had to write the story to fit the illustrations?

A Yes, it was quite hard.

Q Do you think illustrations help you to 'see' a story better?

A Yes. For example, if a story is about a long dark classroom, like one of Roald Dahl's stories I can think of, the illustrator can include things in his picture which aren't in the story.

Q So the illustration 'fills in' some things which the story doesn't give you?

A Yes.

'The FBIZ' (*Gareth*)

'I like fantasy books and Roald Dahl's books and you can pick up tips from them to use when you write your own.

The story is about a boy who finds an aeroplane which he learns to fly but then, in the end, he has to give it back to the airforce.

In a good illustration you can imagine that you're inside the place illustrated. In the film 'Never Ending Story', a boy reads a book and then imagines he's in the story. Sometimes with really good illustrations they can actually make you feel you're seeing the real thing.'

(*Catherine*)

'Sometimes I think it's good not to have illustrations so that you can invent the story in your own mind. But illustrations help you to see what's in an artist's mind. So if you are reading a story and then turn the page you can see if your idea is anything like that of the artist.'

(*Christine*)

'I like adventure stories.'

Q   Does reading influence your writing?
A   I think it helps with the wording and getting the expressions of people talking in your stories right.

'The Bowler Hat' (*David*)

'It's about a boy who finds an old bowler hat by the side of the road and he had to keep it from scientists who are trying to take it. It's a very valuable hat worn by King Henry in the seventeenth century. So the boy took it to the museum to keep it safe but a scientist there tries to steal it but it was safely looked after in the end.

I like watching cartoons on TV and then I try to draw them from memory.'

(*Paul*)

'I sometimes had difficulty in finding something on the page of writing I could draw, so in the end I took some small part of the story and illustrated that. It makes you use your imagination if you're stuck like that.'

By the fourth week the writing was completed and the illustrations matching each page of writing, drawn with pencil crayon and pen, were at the finishing stages. The penultimate process was designing the title page and making front and rear covers (it must be remembered that whereas Western bindings have one completed hinged cover, Eastern bindings have two independent covers). The inside fold of the outer covers became a decorative area, setting off the facing title page. In one case, where the book comprised several stories, a list of contents was placed on the reverse of the title page. The cover designs and title page were all afforded the same attention as the story and illustrations. I made sketches on the board suggesting ways in which cover title, author and artwork could be juxtaposed into an integrated design. We looked at different kinds of letterface designs and discussed the appropriateness of letter design to story content. A ghostly story might require different letter shapes to a science fiction story set on Mars. Similarly, the cover artwork had not only to reflect the story behind it but attract the eye to it. I knew that much more time was needed on these important book art aspects than I had allowed. My dilemma was whether to prolong the project and give detailed attention to design, or to terminate the production at this level of understanding. I chose the latter because, relying on instinct, I felt that the book concept had been taken as far as was appropriate at that time. The attention it deserved would accumulate over a period of time.

The final process was pagination – ensuring the pages were in the right order – and then binding, using bulldog clips or the home-made presses to secure the loose pages before stitching. I demonstrated the authentic Japanese four-hole binding technique but I gave the class freedom to determine the number and arrangement of binding holes as they wished. I thought it would personalise the process if pupils made their own pattern of holes thus creating a hall-mark signature of their own. Distances between holes were measured and most children found little difficulty in using the awl to make holes through the layers of paper before the stitching. The stitching, though, proved harder, for, whilst European binding follows a simple over-under pattern, side-binding can be more complex, especially if an elaborate pattern is sewn. However, although a fixed sewing pattern can be imposed, almost any route can be taken, for one is sure to finish up eventually where one started and tie a knot! Perhaps the free spirit within me prefers this course of non-specific action, because, as an incurable empiricist, I believe that trial and error is by far the best educator.

Some children, as might be expected, were

Japanese side binding

BEFORE YOU BEGIN YOU WILL NEED A PRESS :–
(1) WOOD PRESS (FOR A4 FOLDED TO A5).

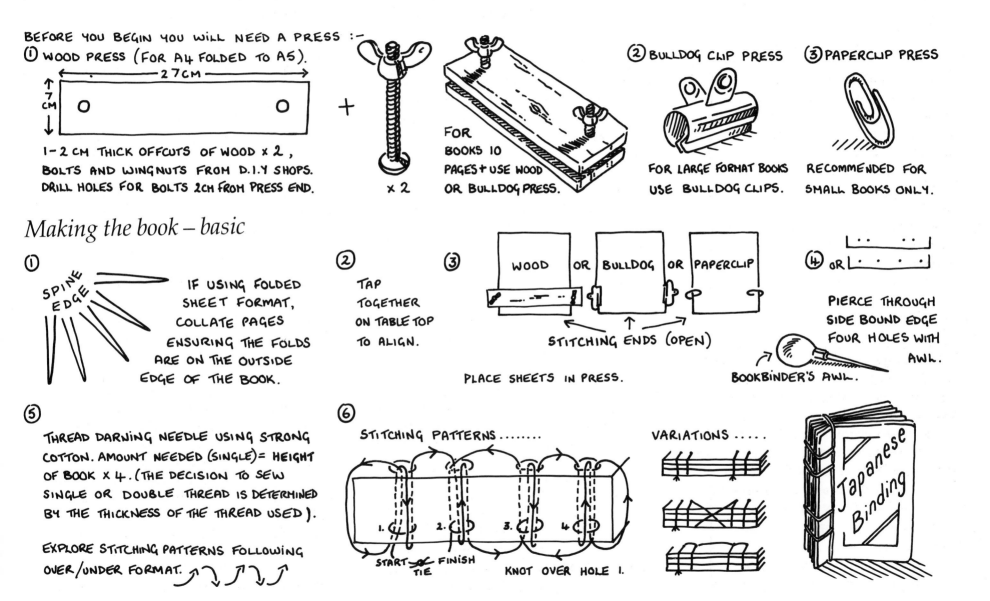

←————— 27CM —————→

↑7CM↓

1–2 CM THICK OFFCUTS OF WOOD × 2,
BOLTS AND WINGNUTS FROM D.I.Y SHOPS.
DRILL HOLES FOR BOLTS 2CM FROM PRESS END.

× 2

FOR BOOKS 10 PAGES + USE WOOD OR BULLDOG PRESS.

(2) BULLDOG CLIP PRESS

FOR LARGE FORMAT BOOKS USE BULLDOG CLIPS.

(3) PAPERCLIP PRESS

RECOMMENDED FOR SMALL BOOKS ONLY.

Making the book – basic

(1) SPINE EDGE

IF USING FOLDED SHEET FORMAT, COLLATE PAGES ENSURING THE FOLDS ARE ON THE OUTSIDE EDGE OF THE BOOK.

(2) TAP TOGETHER ON TABLE TOP TO ALIGN.

(3) WOOD OR BULLDOG OR PAPERCLIP

STITCHING ENDS (OPEN)

PLACE SHEETS IN PRESS.

(4) or

PIERCE THROUGH SIDE BOUND EDGE FOUR HOLES WITH AWL.

BOOKBINDER'S AWL.

(5) THREAD DARNING NEEDLE USING STRONG COTTON. AMOUNT NEEDED (SINGLE) = HEIGHT OF BOOK × 4. (THE DECISION TO SEW SINGLE OR DOUBLE THREAD IS DETERMINED BY THE THICKNESS OF THE THREAD USED).

EXPLORE STITCHING PATTERNS FOLLOWING OVER/UNDER FORMAT.

(6) STITCHING PATTERNS ....

1. 2. 3. 4.

START TIE FINISH

KNOT OVER HOLE 1.

VARIATIONS .....

Japanese Binding

103

Japanese side binding – hard cover

1 Open (4 section)

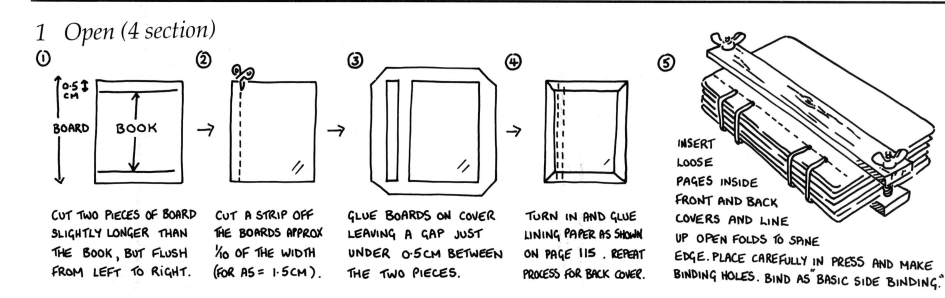

①
0.5 CM
BOARD | BOOK

CUT TWO PIECES OF BOARD SLIGHTLY LONGER THAN THE BOOK, BUT FLUSH FROM LEFT TO RIGHT.

② CUT A STRIP OFF THE BOARDS APPROX ¹/₁₀ OF THE WIDTH (FOR A5 = 1.5CM).

③ GLUE BOARDS ON COVER LEAVING A GAP JUST UNDER 0.5CM BETWEEN THE TWO PIECES.

④ TURN IN AND GLUE LINING PAPER AS SHOWN ON PAGE 115. REPEAT PROCESS FOR BACK COVER.

⑤ INSERT LOOSE PAGES INSIDE FRONT AND BACK COVERS AND LINE UP OPEN FOLDS TO SPINE EDGE. PLACE CAREFULLY IN PRESS AND MAKE BINDING HOLES. BIND AS "BASIC SIDE BINDING."

2 Closed (5 section)

THIS PROCESS IS SIMILAR TO THE ABOVE METHOD EXCEPT A SPINE IS ADDED AND THE BOOK IS THEREFORE CLOSED AT THE SPINE.

FOLLOW THE ABOVE PROCEDURE FOR STAGES ① + ② THEN ADD ANOTHER STRIP THE SAME LENGTH AS THE OTHER TWO PIECES ③. THE SPINE'S WIDTH IS DETERMINED BY THE NUMBER OF PAGES IN THE BOOK WHICH SHOULD BE APPROXIMATELY THE WIDTH OF THE BOOKS PAGES × 2.

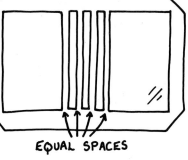

④ EQUAL SPACES

ATTACH BOARDS AND LEAVE SAME SPACES AS "OPEN BINDING" ABOVE.

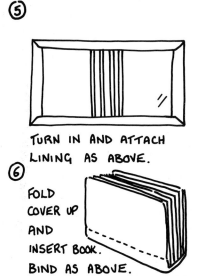

⑤ TURN IN AND ATTACH LINING AS ABOVE.

⑥ FOLD COVER UP AND INSERT BOOK. BIND AS ABOVE.

POEMS OF FUJI

3 Three section cover book

Hard cover book

This method is very adaptable to large scale work. The design here is for A4 format single horizontal sheet (unfolded.)

①
30.05CM | 22 CM | BACK COVER | A4

LAY A4 PAPER ON BOARD FLUSH TO LEFT AND APPROX 0.5CM MARGIN ON THE OTHER THREE SIDES.

②
2 | 22 CM | 28CM | FRONT COVER

CUT TWO PIECES OF CARD AS SHOWN.

③
BACK

ATTACH BACK BOARD TO COVER PAPER AND LAY LINING AS SHOWN ON PAGE 115.

④
0.5CM | FRONT

REPEAT PROCESS FOR FRONT COVER ALLOWING 0.5CM GAP BETWEEN THE TWO PIECES.

⑤
INSERT A4 BOOK INTO COVERS SO THAT SPINE SIDE EDGES ALIGN. FASTEN WITH BULLDOG CLIPS.

⑥
PIERCE HOLES IN THE GAP AND SEW AS FOR "OPEN SIDE BINDING."

⑦
IN THIS FORM OF SIDE BINDING ONLY THE LARGER SECTION OF THE COVER OPENS WHILST THE BACK REMAINS STATIONARY.

A BOOK of TREES

Soft cover book

①
30.05 CM | 22 CM | BACK = A4 | 0.5 CM

USING THICK CARD CUT BACK COVER AS ABOVE.

②
FRONT

CUT FRONT COVER TO SAME MEASUREMENTS AND SCORE 2.05 CM IN FROM LEFT SIDE.

③
TURN FRONT COVER OVER SO THAT SCORED SECTION WILL OPEN OUTWARDS. FASTEN AND SEW AS BEFORE.

AS A TEMPORARY WAY OF HOLDING A MOCK-UP BOOK TOGETHER, USE PAPERCLIPS TO HOLD UNSEWN BOOK TOGETHER.

handier than others at sewing. Some produced intricate woven patterns of near embroidery, and others found even single hole tying almost an impossibility. Using double thread produced its own problems (as always) especially when 'pulling through' the thread, a process which tends to create a little bundle of knots. The way to avoid this it to pull through the thread slowly, checking for the formation of knots or, ideally, for a partner to hold the thread taut as it is pulled through. Knot tying itself, of course, created problems but working in pairs, each borrowing the other's finger, when required, helped.

The sewing was by far the most exasperating part of the whole book production. Several children made many attempts at getting the sewing right, and I tuned my ears to detect noises of despair which, decoded, said 'Help!' Fortunately, not more than four or five children finished the pagination at the same time so there was no rush on the limited presses, clips, awls and needles at my disposal.

I should add that before the final binding took place all the books were photocopied in their loose, open A4 format and then bound as the originals. In this way, whoever retained the original, other interested parties like myself could have a copy. It is worth emphasising here that black ink gives a much sharper reproduction than dark blue – a point worth remembering if photocopying books is envisaged.

The side-binding project had taken four to five mornings to complete (although David was still working on his book three weeks after everyone else had finished theirs). Most children had shown themselves capable of putting a story together. The shortest book comprised three pages of writing; the largest eight; the average five. The longest stories were not necessarily the best and many lacked a well-shaped plot, with an inclination to 'jump' from one situation to another without 'stepping stones' and for endings to be sudden and unresolved. Illustrations varied too, and were conceptually weaker than the writing. Pupils easily fell back on stereotyped images gleaned from popular sources. The decorative elements of the cover designs, more a preoccupation at the expense of design, probably came from pattern work in

Carefully folding pages from A4 to A5

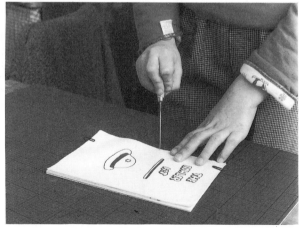

Using bookbinder's awl to pierce holes for four-hole binding (paperclip press)

Stitching four-hole side binding

earlier years. But I was generally satisfied with the results. It was, after all, their first ever self-made book and their enthusiasm and commitment had been enlightening.

In all the book art production done so far with children, I had not employed the European central binding technique using hard covers. Whether or not this was an oversight I am uncertain; somehow the need for it hadn't really arisen. I have already said that traditional bookbinding in the classroom can be deadly, and perhaps it was for this reason that, unconsciously, I had sidetracked it for alternative routes to book art.

Somewhere, from a voice within, came the call to spend my last major project with children exploring European hard cover binding, or rather an adaption of it to suit the needs of children.

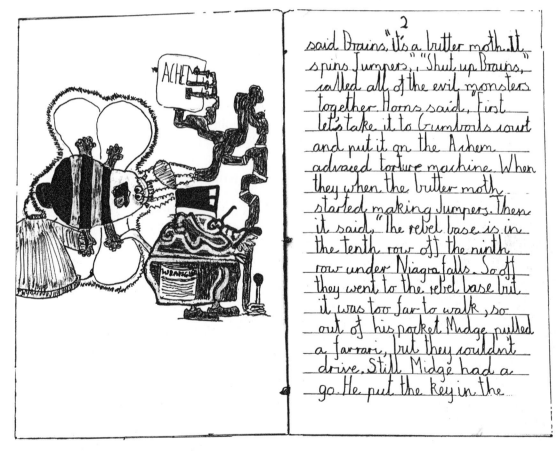

Magnus decided to break with tradition and stitch a three-hole pattern

Books with hard covers

This next activity was carried out with the sixth year of Brookburn Primary School. The strategy was for pupils to work in pairs. This provides a number of advantages: shared ideas in story writing often produce surprising and unexpected solutions to plot development. As in conversation, a wholly original way of looking at a situation can be experienced. Our imagination is as much a prison as a source of revelation. A 'lost' or 'stuck' story can be revitalised by the involvement of another author. Another advantage of shared working is that the process, from conception to completion, is quickened. There is less likelihood that the story will lose its impetus, specially towards the end. Also, pupils' strengths can be utilised to the full; tasks delegated to match preferences and aptitudes, for example writing, illustration, design, lettering. But essentially it is the social element which is so important here. The skills of working as a team, organising a working structure and solving problems jointly as they arrive. The class was arranged into friendship pairs and a group improvisation set in motion.

It was agreed that the book would comprise ten pages arranged on six A5 leaves folded from three A4 sheets of cartridge paper (plus an endpaper page). Several book simulations and blackboard graphics illustrated the chronological sequence of endpaper (later to be glued to the cover), title pages, text and

Group improvisation

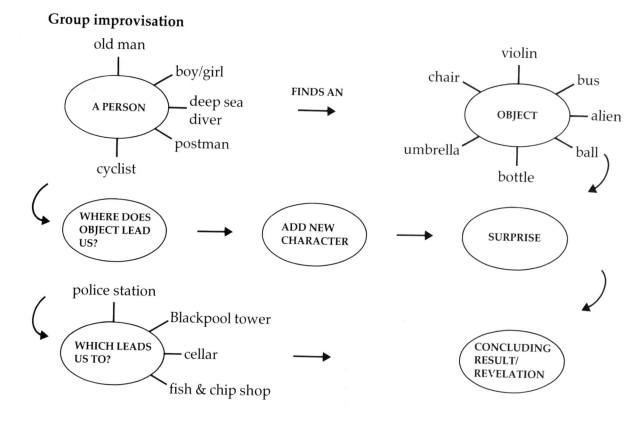

illustrations. Writing was designated to left side pages (1, 3, 5, 7, 9) and illustrations to right side pages (2, 4, 6, 8, 10).

The usefulness of these blackboard graphics was to suggest the number of sentences appropriate to the story form, for example if a page was half writing and half blank space, this would imply, say, three sentences. Using this technique, the whole story could be allocated to the five writing pages even before the writing of the first draft had begun. Writing a story to fit a book, rather than the more usual way of fitting a book around a story, is a technique I discussed earlier. I so often observe children writing stories in book form without any real concept of the book itself. This can result in an unsatisfactory presentation, like, for example, words being

Book pages

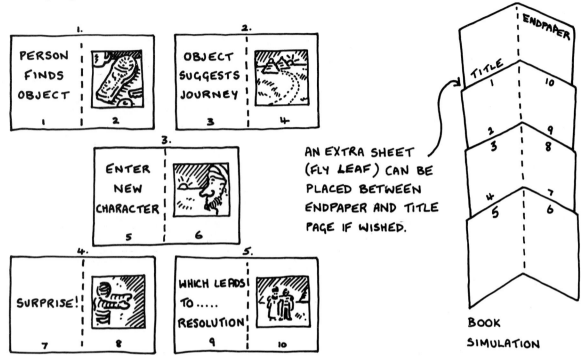

1. PERSON FINDS OBJECT — 1, 2

2. OBJECT SUGGESTS JOURNEY — 3, 4

3. ENTER NEW CHARACTER — 5, 6

4. SURPRISE! — 7, 8

5. WHICH LEADS TO..... RESOLUTION — 9, 10

AN EXTRA SHEET (FLY LEAF) CAN BE PLACED BETWEEN ENDPAPER AND TITLE PAGE IF WISHED.

ENDPAPER
TITLE
1 10
2 9
3 8
4 7
5 6

BOOK SIMULATION

squeezed together because the page space is inadequate. The European bound book is a special problem because unlike concertina and side-bound books, the structure is from the centre outwards. Careful planning is necessary if a book of too many or too few pages is to be avoided.

From this beginning, the pair-drafting began. If pupil 'A' was responsible for writing, pupil 'B' would draft artwork, whilst both being responsible for the story. When an episode was too long to fit on the page, aesthetically, the pair set about extracting the essence of it and reduced it accordingly.

If too few words were forthcoming, either discussion was required to enlarge the plot or artwork/design incorporated instead. As only one of the pair could work on the book page at any one time, it was decided to present finished writing on separate paper to be pasted into the book on completion. This enabled the illustration of the book to progress unhindered. The corrected rough drafts were exchanged, read, criticised and final presentation applied to fit the A5 format.

Jack produced some of the most satisfying illustrations. The centre page drawing of Jack's part of the story includes a careful study of his own left hand. Suzanne's centre page spread is a successful arrangement of shapes, textures and text. The path logically carried the eye across the page.

As the books were completed, a title page design was produced for the reverse side of page one, and finally a blank sheet of A4 wrapped around the completed storybook. (This would later be glued down to the cover boards.)

My original aim had been for the pupils to cut their own cover boards, but with ever-decreasing time available for the project, I did this myself. Medium weight cartridge paper was cut to a dimension approximately 2 cm larger than the cover board and spine dimensions. This became the book cover. Diagrams went on the board showing how the cover design would fit on to the book when finished. It was still difficult for many pupils to conceive the flat sheet of paper as a three-dimensional book cover. An important factor was that the parameter of the cover, a 2 cm margin, would eventually be folded over and glued down to the inside cover boards. This was not clearly understood by some pupils, placing titles too high, and then finding the tops of letters disappearing over the top edge of the cover boards.

Page from 'The Return of the Bottle' by Ben and Jack (11)

Page from 'The Drawing Pin' by Suzanne and Carolyn (11)

The next stage was the stitching. I demonstrated a conventional five hole over/under stitching pattern. One of the advantages of pupils working at varying speeds is that the demand on tools and equipment like darning needles can be eased. As groups of four to six children finished the presentation I could show them the stitching technique again, this time at close quarters and give advice individually.

The cover design had to take into account front and back covers, spine and fold-over margins. It was possible, however, for the spinal title to be done after the final assembly,

and some pupils did this, although it does require very dexterous penmanship. I showed the class professionally designed book covers so they could see:

1. how the essence of the story contained within the book is expressed in the cover design;
2. that through colour and the arrangement of shapes the eye is attracted to the book by its cover;
3. that the words are an integral part of the design; and
4. that lettering is an art form.

Both book artists, I thought, should work on the cover design, and although this was a relatively small area, this did not prove too great a difficulty. Artwork tended to be shared, but some pairs like Ben and Jack decided to delegate artwork and lettering as separate tasks.

The next stage was the placing of the cover boards on the reverse side of the cover design. Traditionally, children have been required to paste down the whole of the cover paper to the boards. I have never done this with any of my own books, or found it necessary. In fact I find the less adhesive used the better. It is my practice to use a tiny dot of adhesive on the centre of the cover boards and spine, and this just holds it in place on the cover paper. Providing the turned-in cover is securely attached, the book is as secure as any other method of book binding. This is the procedure I used with the children. Next the corner mitres are cut, the turned-in flaps brushed along the edges with adhesive and pressed firmly down to the cover boards. This was demonstrated to small groups as they neared this stage of the production. I cut a mitre from one of the corners of the cover paper freehand, using my eye to judge the 45° angle. I wondered if I could expect this of the children (and indeed if they should use knives at all) but as they were closely supervised I took the risk and was delighted with the result. They did some test runs first, practising eye-measured 45° angles on odd paper fragments until they felt able to attend to the cover mitres. They did this accurately and cleanly, with the precision of a surgeon, remembering to leave a gap the thickness of the cover board at the corner. (With thin cover paper it is possible to avoid cutting mitres and to simply fold the corners into the boards; however, with heavier paper, like the cartridge we were using, this method would have produced an unpleasant bulge at the corners, so was best avoided.)

It is for the class teacher, with his/her knowledge of the individual pupils, to decide what the teacher does, and what can be reasonably expected of the children. The

The cover design after binding. The original design was 2 cm larger than the cover boards to allow for 'turning-in'

'The Drawing Pin' by Suzanne and Carolyn

mitres can be cut with scissors, but as the paper is best left flat, cutting with a knife on a cutting mat is preferable.

Here again, I must confess to not keeping to the traditional roles of book binding. The process I have described so far is largely a 'rule of eye' method because this is the way I make my own books. I 'measure' hardly anything – using my eye to sense accuracy. If the cover boards, the spine, the gaps between them, and the thickness of the boards were all mechanically measured then the exact size of the cover paper could be calculated and the cover cut to size. The mitres could then be cut using scissors in a normally held position. Some teachers may wish to do this and indeed

see it as a mathematical skill exercise. I fully endorse this approach but it is not the way I wish to work with children. I have developed a very keen eye and try to evolve the same skills in those I teach. It is after all the oldest skill of all, an innate skill known to every African tribesman but largely lost to our own society which relies for nearly everything on mechanical devices.

As each pair of book artists came to me ready for the joining of the book to its cover I adopted the following procedure: I turned in the top, longer fold and glued it over the head.

Hard cover binding for concertina and European style books

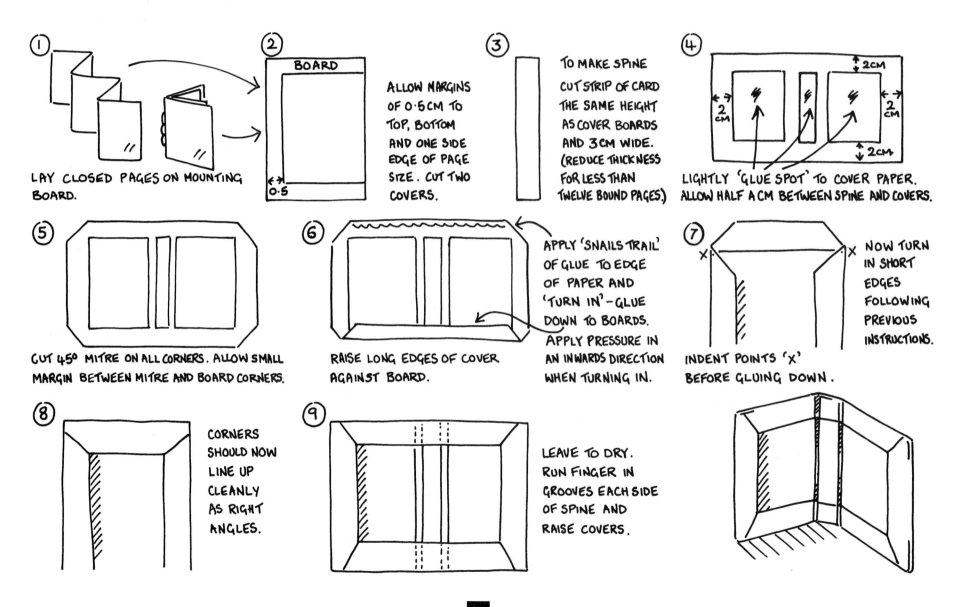

① LAY CLOSED PAGES ON MOUNTING BOARD.

② ALLOW MARGINS OF 0·5CM TO TOP, BOTTOM AND ONE SIDE EDGE OF PAGE SIZE. CUT TWO COVERS.
BOARD
0·5

③ TO MAKE SPINE CUT STRIP OF CARD THE SAME HEIGHT AS COVER BOARDS AND 3CM WIDE. (REDUCE THICKNESS FOR LESS THAN TWELVE BOUND PAGES.)

④ LIGHTLY 'GLUE SPOT' TO COVER PAPER. ALLOW HALF A CM BETWEEN SPINE AND COVERS.
2CM 2CM 2CM 2CM

⑤ CUT 45° MITRE ON ALL CORNERS. ALLOW SMALL MARGIN BETWEEN MITRE AND BOARD CORNERS.

⑥ RAISE LONG EDGES OF COVER AGAINST BOARD.
APPLY 'SNAILS TRAIL' OF GLUE TO EDGE OF PAPER AND 'TURN IN' - GLUE DOWN TO BOARDS. APPLY PRESSURE IN AN INWARDS DIRECTION WHEN TURNING IN.

⑦ INDENT POINTS 'X' BEFORE GLUING DOWN.
NOW TURN IN SHORT EDGES FOLLOWING PREVIOUS INSTRUCTIONS.

⑧ CORNERS SHOULD NOW LINE UP CLEANLY AS RIGHT ANGLES.

⑨ LEAVE TO DRY. RUN FINGER IN GROOVES EACH SIDE OF SPINE AND RAISE COVERS.

Joining pages to cover – open style binding

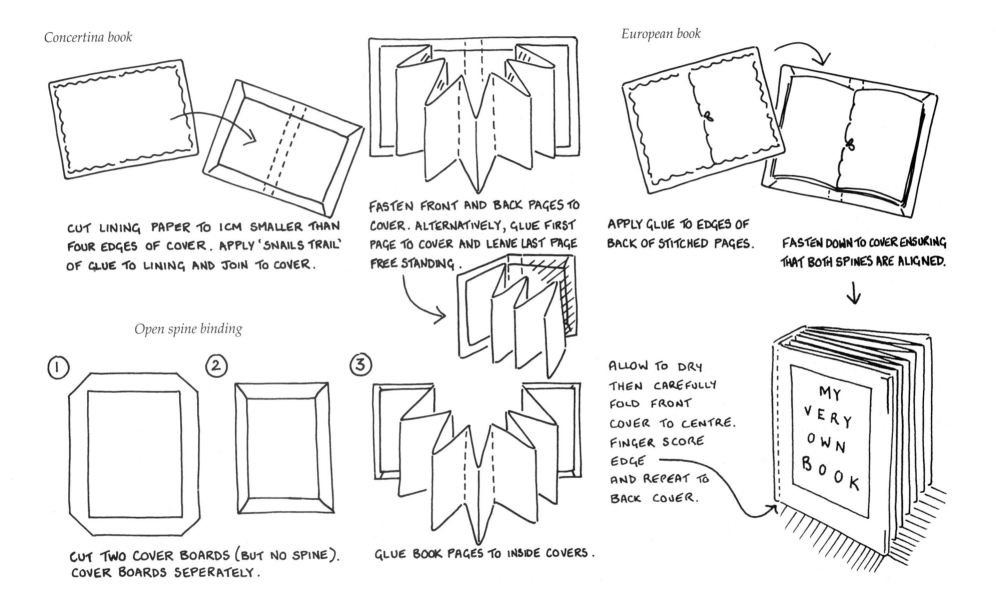

Concertina book

CUT LINING PAPER TO 1CM SMALLER THAN FOUR EDGES OF COVER. APPLY 'SNAILS TRAIL' OF GLUE TO LINING AND JOIN TO COVER.

FASTEN FRONT AND BACK PAGES TO COVER. ALTERNATIVELY, GLUE FIRST PAGE TO COVER AND LEAVE LAST PAGE FREE STANDING.

Open spine binding

① ② ③

CUT TWO COVER BOARDS (BUT NO SPINE). COVER BOARDS SEPERATELY.

GLUE BOOK PAGES TO INSIDE COVERS.

European book

APPLY GLUE TO EDGES OF BACK OF STITCHED PAGES.

FASTEN DOWN TO COVER ENSURING THAT BOTH SPINES ARE ALIGNED.

ALLOW TO DRY THEN CAREFULLY FOLD FRONT COVER TO CENTRE. FINGER SCORE EDGE AND REPEAT TO BACK COVER.

MY VERY OWN BOOK

European binding

Soft cover

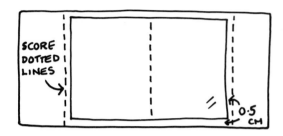

FOLLOW BASIC BINDING TO STITCHING STAGE THEN LAY BOOK ON CARTRIDGE SHEET. ALLOW 0.5CM MARGIN TOP AND BOTTOM AND ENOUGH MARGIN LEFT AND RIGHT TO FOLD IN AS COVER FLAPS.

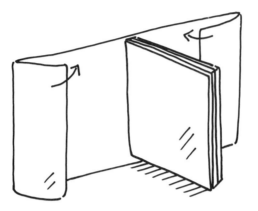

STITCH AS FOR BASIC BOOK BUT START ON INSIDE AND THUS TIE KNOT INSIDE OF SPINE.

Card cover

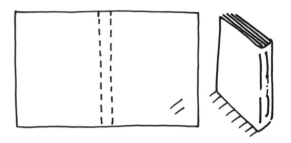

BASICALLY THE SAME TECHNIQUE CAN BE APPLIED TO A CARD COVER. SCORE SPINE x 2 WIDTHS OF BOOK + FOLLOW PROCEDURE FOR SOFT COVER BOOK.

Additions to bound books

FOLDING PAGE WITH PAPER CLASP.

PAGE WITH FLAPS.

CONCERTINA BOOK BOUND INTO CENTRALLY BOUND BOOK.

MULTI-FORMED BOOK.

PAGE WITH POCKETS

OPENING OUT MAP OR DIAGRAM.

Decorative binding features

Sewing decorative scrolls of paper on the spine of soft covered books can add to their attraction. Cut a strip of paper approximately 10 cm long × 3 cm wide and roll it evenly on a nail. Glue edge down. Make more scrolls, perhaps using different colours or textures of paper. When stitching, thread these scrolls so that they appear on the outer edge of the spine between the holes.

Variation

Cut a wedge out of the centre of the spine and pages. Stitch spine and include a scroll in the middle 'hole' area.

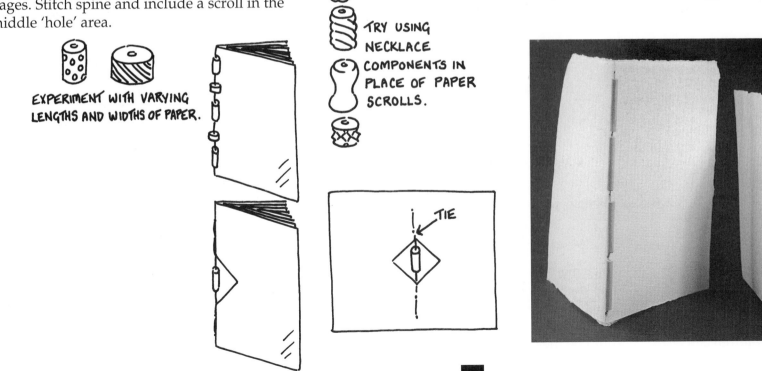

GLUE

TRY USING NECKLACE COMPONENTS IN PLACE OF PAPER SCROLLS.

EXPERIMENT WITH VARYING LENGTHS AND WIDTHS OF PAPER.

TIE

Cover decorations

Contemporary designer bookbinders like to use all manner of objects as relief forms on the cover of books. Indeed the books of some modern designer bookbinders like Philip Smith look like sculptures. Children can also experiment with gluing flattish natural and man-made objects on their covers. Of course, they should reflect the theme of the book in some way. An unusual stimulus for a story could be the objects glued on the cover, so that a comb, milk bottle top and a shoe lace would have to be incorporated into the plot. None of the books shown here have titles on their covers. Do you think that this adds to their attraction or detracts from it?

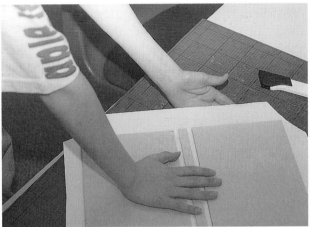

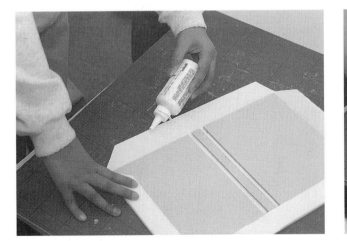

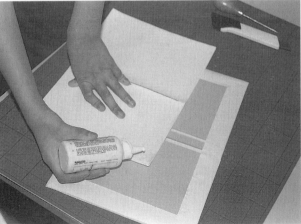

Always use minimum adhesive (don't feel you must apply it thickly because if you do, it will all flood out when you 'press down' and give you the unnecessary task of cleaning it all off later). I then gently but firmly press the strip down to the cover boards from the head-edge inwards (to press or apply pressure in any other direction will almost certainly create creases). It is important to run one's finger and apply pressure along the point at which the paper crosses the edge of the board as one attaches the flap down. if this is not done a gap usually appears between board and cover which is untidy in appearance. One of the pair then proceeded to turn in the shorter, left fold and fastened it over the fore-edge following my example. The remaining pupil did the same to the right fold and then one of us completed the turning-in by glueing the bottom fold over the tail. If these folds are not satisfactorily completed they can carefully be peeled free again, providing only a short time has elapsed since glueing. The old adhesive can be peeled off, a new layer applied and the turning-in tried a second (and hopefully final) time.

Finally, in this seemingly complex set of procedures comes the attaching of the single section book to the completed cover.

My own method, with all but the smallest books, is to apply the adhesive to the spine of the book first and then along the three edges of the left endpaper; align the book vertically and horizontally to cover and then lower book to cover; open to centre page and press firmly down to spine; open quickly to left endpaper and run fingers down the spine and the outwards/upwards to head of endpaper, outwards/downwards to tail, and outwards across to the fore-edge. When pressing down the endpapers always spread in an outwards direction. Now it is the turn of the right side of the book which should be processed in the same way. Lining up the book to the cover can be difficult. First-attempt books are sometimes spoilt because the pages are 'out of true' with the cover. If this happens, all is not lost if you act quickly. Gently peel away the endpaper from the cover, and, providing the adhesive has not yet coagulated, it is still possible to reset. With these children I glued the spine and left endpaper, placed the book on the cover but let the pupils press down the spine and endpaper. They then repeated this on the other side of the book but this time they were responsible for both glueing and pressing down.

The completed book was then left to set for a few minutes. All that remains to be done at this stage is for the front cover to be raised carefully to the vertical position. As this is done the index finger of the right hand should gently score the spine edge of the endpaper. This prevents the endpaper bubbling up

under the pressure of being raised. The same should be done to the back cover. On the outside of the book gently indent (with the finger tip) the cover paper into the spinal grooves. This gives a pleasing raised effect to the spine. Needless to say the hand should be clean for these final stages. Any surplus adhesive to be found can be carefully cleaned when set. (I think it only fair to repeat that much of what I have suggested runs contrary to traditional school book binding practice; it is very much a 'personal view' not an orthodox methodology.)

As one by one the books were finished, the room vibrated with a wonderful sense of accomplishment. Yet still a critical eye prevailed. Discrepancies previously concealed in the 'becoming' process now became noticeable. Cover designs conceived in the flat looked different when folded so extra artwork was sometimes applied. Title pages were less convincing than at first thought, endpapers and fly leaves looked in need of some kind of decoration.

The books were passed around the room to be viewed, read and 'experienced', for the books were objects of aesthetic meaning independent of what they contained. When a few days later they were covered in acetate film to protect them, the books on display aroused more interest than all the school library books put together.

It had been yet another crash programme. My most ambitious book project achieved in four to five afternoons. Not surprisingly, all

manner of imperfections are evident in them from story, grammar, handwriting to cover design and binding. But to have entered this hard cover book project at a deeper, more prolonged level of expectation would not have been a success. Had I been able to work with them all week, over a longer period of time, and had it not been the summer term, increasingly reaching its far end, my tactics would have been different. But the advantage of this truncated project was that it provided evidence that a book, and a well-made book at that, complete in every way with story and illustrations can be made by children (with some assistance) in a very limited and fragmented period of time.

⑧ Other types of books

Computerised books

No book artist is complete without informational technology skills. The access to writing that computerised story making makes available is essential to language development far beyond the immediate confines of this book. Here are just three examples of word-processed books.

'The Adventures of Furry the Gerbil' by Christopher and Daniel (infants). This comprises five pages of print supported by artwork. The computer printout has been attached to lightweight cartridge holding the artwork on the reverse side. An extended left-hand margin has enabled binding by the side-bound method.

'Our Minibeast Hunt' is a collection of poems written (and word-processed) in pairs by middle juniors. The poems are beautifully mounted with illustrations, and the whole is bound as a concertina book in hard covers.

'3C Strikes Again' by Emma (top junior) is an arrangement of computer processed text and illustration. The book was designed around the printout material, centrally bound, and then text and illustration pasted into the pages.

'The Adventures of Furry the Gerbil' by Christopher and Daniel

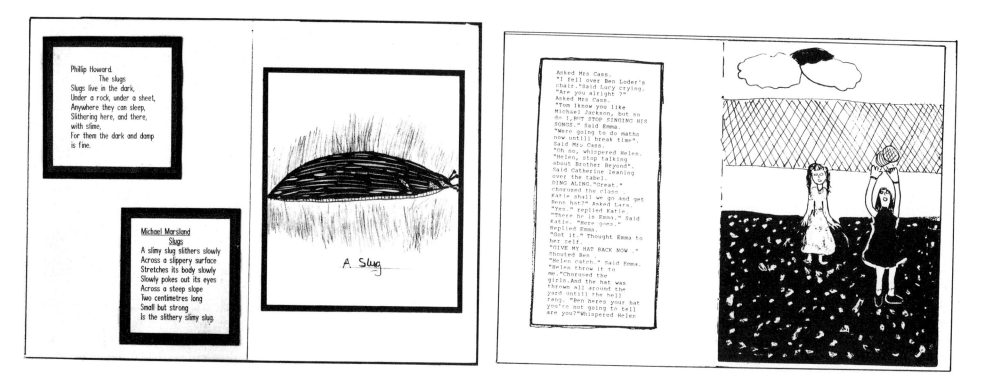

Phillip Howard.
      The slugs
Slugs live in the dark,
Under a rock, under a sheet,
Anywhere they can sleep,
Slithering here, and there,
with slime,
For them the dark and damp
is fine.

Michael Marsland
Slugs
A slimy slug slithers slowly
Across a slippery surface
Stretches its body slowly
Slowly pokes out its eyes
Across a steep slope
Two centimetres long
Small but strong
Is the slithery slimy slug.

A. Slug

Asked Mrs Cass.
"I fell over Ben Loder's
chair."Said Lucy crying.
"Are you alright ?"
Asked Mrs Cass.
"Tom Iknow you like
Michael Jackson, but so
do I,BUT STOP SINGING HIS
SONGS." Said Emma.
"Were going to do maths
now untill break time".
Said Mrs Cass.
"Oh no, whispered Helen.
"Helen, stop talking
about Brother Beyond".
Said Catherine leaning
over the tabel.
DING ALING."Great."
chorused the class
Katie shall we go and get
Bens hat?" Asked Lara.
"Yes." replied Katie.
"There he is Emma." Said
Katie. "Here goes."
Replied Emma.
"Got it." Thought Emma to
her self.
"GIVE MY HAT BACK NOW ."
Shouted Ben .
"Helen catch." Said Emma.
"Helen throw it to
me."Chorused the
girls.And the hat was
thrown all around the
yard untill the bell
rang. "Ben heres your hat
you're not going to tell
are you?"Whispered Helen

'Our Minibeast Hunt'

'3C Strikes Again'

Theme books

Theme books enable a class topic to be bound together. Not only are they hugely popular with children, they can become useful resource material in the classroom, decorate wall spaces if hung, and provide an effective protection of children's work to be stored.

All the binding methods already discussed can be employed, although there is a tendency for books to be of a larger format than individual books.

'Feel' book (side-bound) (Nursery)

Large format side-bound theme book. Black sugar paper was folded in half to make pages and the complete book stitched with wool (Infants)

The pages of this A1 size book were joined together by a paper strip and the ends bound as an 'open' concertina book using paper covered boards (Infants)

In this theme book each child in the class was given a letter of the alphabet to draw using words beginning with the appropriate letter as the source of visual imagery e.g. 'O' = Octopus, 'P' = Plant (Year four – side-bound on unfolded A1 sheets)

'The Tree' – Poems and observational drawings (Year three)

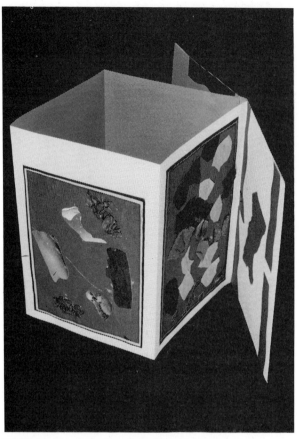 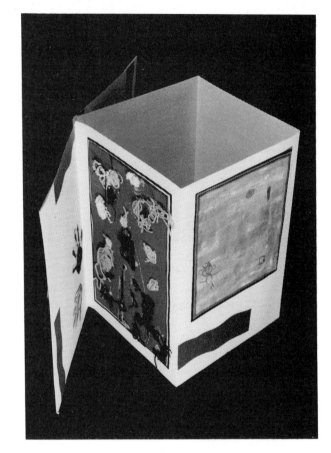

3D Theme book on the colour blue (Nursery)

Appendix 1 – General information on making books

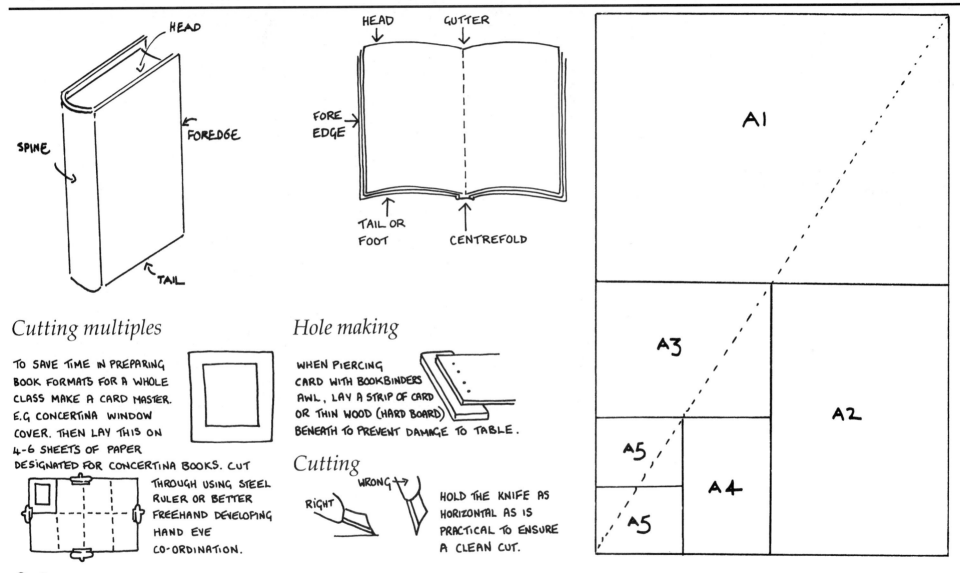

HEAD

FOREDGE

SPINE

TAIL

HEAD **GUTTER**

FORE EDGE

TAIL OR FOOT **CENTREFOLD**

Cutting multiples

TO SAVE TIME IN PREPARING BOOK FORMATS FOR A WHOLE CLASS MAKE A CARD MASTER. E.G CONCERTINA WINDOW COVER. THEN LAY THIS ON 4-6 SHEETS OF PAPER DESIGNATED FOR CONCERTINA BOOKS. CUT THROUGH USING STEEL RULER OR BETTER FREEHAND DEVELOPING HAND EYE CO-ORDINATION.

Hole making

WHEN PIERCING CARD WITH BOOKBINDERS AWL, LAY A STRIP OF CARD OR THIN WOOD (HARD BOARD) BENEATH TO PREVENT DAMAGE TO TABLE.

Cutting

RIGHT **WRONG**

HOLD THE KNIFE AS HORIZONTAL AS IS PRACTICAL TO ENSURE A CLEAN CUT.

A1

A3

A2

A5

A4

A5

USE COLOURED COTTONS + THREADS TO MAKE THE SEWN PARTS OF THE BOOK MORE VISUALLY PLEASING.

Cutting page edges

TO AVOID RAISED CENTRAL FOREDGES IN BOUND BOOK,

LAY STEEL RULER ALONG EDGE OF PROTRUDING PAGES AND CUT THROUGH.

OR IF PAGES PROTRUDE BEYOND COVERS............

'Making a slip case'

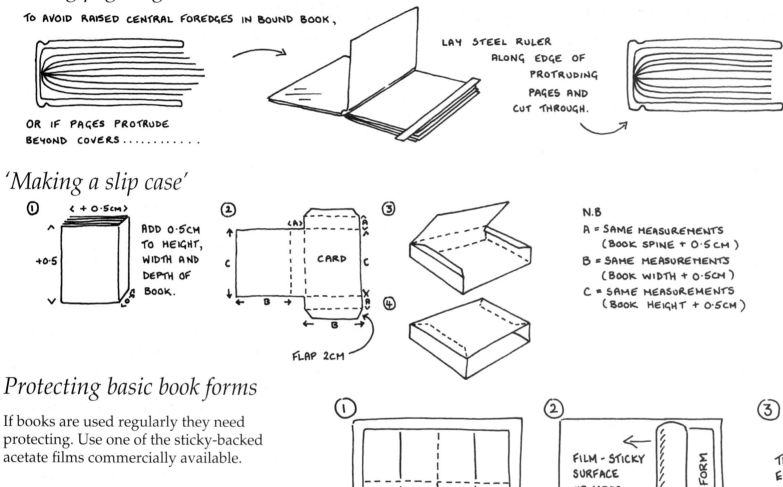

① < + 0.5CM >

+0.5

ADD 0.5CM TO HEIGHT, WIDTH AND DEPTH OF BOOK.

② CARD
A
C   C
B
FLAP 2CM

③

④

N.B

A = SAME MEASUREMENTS (BOOK SPINE + 0.5 CM)

B = SAME MEASUREMENTS (BOOK WIDTH + 0.5CM)

C = SAME MEASUREMENTS (BOOK HEIGHT + 0.5CM)

Protecting basic book forms

If books are used regularly they need protecting. Use one of the sticky-backed acetate films commercially available.

① OPEN BASIC BOOK FORM FLAT. CUT ACETATE FILM SLIGHTLY LARGER THAN BOOK FORM AND PEEL OFF PAPER COVERING.

② FILM - STICKY SURFACE UPWARDS   BOOK FORM

ENSURE THAT THERE ARE NO WRINKLES ON FILM. LAY ONE SHORT EDGE OF OPENED BOOK FORM ON FILM EDGE AND SLOWLY ROLL FORM DOWN OVER FILM.

③ TRIM THE FILM EDGE AND WHERE APPLICABLE RECUT THE BOOK'S PANELS THROUGH THE FILM. REASSEMBLE BOOK.

Paper

Drawing (cartridge) paper can be purchased pure white or in cream or buff shades. Paper in pastel hues, and stronger colours are also manufactured.

Paper 'weights'

Paper is referred to by its 'weight', but a sheet of 'medium' paper is not necessarily thicker than a sheet of 'light weight' paper. However in most cases the greater the weight the thicker the paper. As a general rule use thicker paper as books increase in size. With experience you will learn the best thickness of paper to use for the size of book you want. For books made from A2 and A3 paper size use light to medium (115–150 gsm) weight paper. Thinner paper (100–115 gsm) is suitable for A4 size books. (gsm means 'grammes per square meter'.)

Watercolour paper

For a very special book you might want to use watercolour paper. This is more expensive and of a better quality than most other kinds of paper. It is usually made in a mould and has 'deckle' edges. The surface texture of watercolour paper ranges from smooth (called HP, meaning 'hot pressed') to semi-textured (called Not, meaning 'not hot pressed'), to textured (called Rough). Make sure that it is acid free so that it will not deteriorate with age.

Standard paper proportions

Paper is sold in a bewildering range of sizes, but the 'A' size is becoming a standard measurement and is the one used in this book. A2 size is the most popular size in which paper is packaged although paper cuts to A3 and A4 is also available. However, it is usually more economical to buy A2 size and guillotine the paper down to the required size. Design your book to the dimensions (or divisions) of the paper you buy. Only if you are intending to publish a book on a photocopier does it need to conform to 'A' sizes.

Quantities

Single sheets of paper for making books at home can be purchased from your local art and craft shop (addresses can be found in Yellow Pages). Schools will find it economical to buy in bulk. Drawing paper tends to be packaged in 500 sheets, but some papers (e.g. watercolour paper) will usually be supplied in smaller quantities.

Suppliers

For drawing paper suitable for making books:
NES Arnold Ltd, Ludlow Hill Road, West Bridgford, Nottingham NG2 6HD. Tel: 0115 945 2203. Fax: 0115 945 2326. Catalogue available.

For watercolour paper and high quality cartridge paper:
RK Burt Ltd, 57 Union Street, London SE1 1SG. Tel: 0171 407 6474. Fax: 0171 403 3672. This is a wholesale supplier of paper from all over the world and so consequently paper has to be purchased in largish quantities. Samples and catalogue available. Discount to schools and educational institutions.

For smaller quantities of paper:
Falkiner Fine Papers Ltd, 76 Southampton Row, London WC1 B4AR. Tel: 0171 831 1151. Fax: 0171 430 1248.

For smaller quantities of paper and general art materials:
Paperchase, 213 Tottenham Court Road, London W1P 9AF. Tel: 0171 580 8496. Fax: 0171 637 1225.

Photocopier paper

Most schools will have a regular supplier of photocopier paper. Brightly coloured photocopier paper can be purchased from good stationers.
For craft papers, greetings cards blanks, and display materials:
Craft Creations, Ingersoll House, Delamare Road, Cheshunt, Herts. EN8 9ND. Tel: 01992 781 900. Fax: 01992 634 339. Catalogue available.

Handmade paper

Maureen Richardson is one of Britain's leading paper makers. Send stamped addressed envelope for the list of her handmade plant papers, details of her publications, and paper making courses.
Maureen Richardson, Romilly, Brilley, Hay on Wye. Hereford. HR3 6HE. Tel: 01497 831 546.

Cover boards

Greyboard from NES Arnold (see above):
Medium weight (800 gsm), 63.5 × 76 cm.
Heavy weight (1100 gsm), 63.5 × 76 cm. Both in packs of ten sheets.

Cutting mats

Cutting mats are ideal for cutting paper on and are virtually indestructible.
Small CM 30 (30 × 45 cm)
Medium CM 45 (45 × 60 cm)
Large CM 60 (60 × 90 cm)
Edding (UK) Ltd, Merlin Centre, Acrewood Way, St Albans, Herts AL4 0JY. Tel: 01727 846 688. Fax: 01727 839 970. 33% discount to schools. Catalogue available.

Adhesives

Use PVA adhesive for joining paper. I use NES Arnold's 'Easy clean' (see above).
Tools and thread
Scissors, craft knives, steel safety rulers, large darning needles and strong thread from NES Arnold (see above).

Bookbinders' Awls

Dryad Craft Centre, Reeves Shop, 178 Kensington High Street, London W8 7NX. Tel: 0171 937 5370. Also stocks bookbinding equipment.
Kutrite of Sheffield Ltd, 72 Russell Street, Sheffield S3 8RW. Tel: 0114 273 9977. Fax: 0114 276 8876. Minimum awl order value £25.

Bookbinding

Kojiro Ikegami (1986) *Japanese Bookbinding.* Weatherhill, New York.
The classic primer on Japanese binding techniques.
Pauline Johnson (1963. Reprinted 1990) *Creative Bookbinding.* Dover Publications, New York.

Working with paper

Anne Chambers (1992) *The Practical Guide to Marbling Paper.* Thames and Hudson, London.

Marbled paper is traditionally used to cover and line books. A straight forward handbook of marbling techniques.
Marion Elliot (1997) *Paper Making.* New Holland Ltd, London.
How to make your own paper which can then be used to make books.
Paul Jackson (1991) *The Encyclopedia of Origami and Papercraft Techniques.* Headline, London.
A comprehensive reference book to working with paper. Many useful tips for the book artist here.
Faith Shannon (1987) *The Art and Craft of*

Paper. Mitchell Beazley, London. This accessible handbook includes a section on making and decorating books.

The Book Art Project

For details about The Book Art Project, its courses and publications, contact: Paul Johnson, 11 Hill Top Avenue, Cheadle Hulme, Cheshire, SK8 7HN. Tel: 0161 485 2174.